The
New Directions
Anthology
of Classical
Chinese
Poetry

The
New Directions
Anthology
of Classical
Chinese
Poetry

EDITED BY

Eliot Weinberger

TRANSLATIONS BY

William Carlos Williams

Ezra Pound

Kenneth Rexroth

Gary Snyder

David Hinton

A NEW DIRECTIONS BOOK

This book is dedicated to the memory
of a special New Directions friend, Oliver Gilliland,
one of the best bookmen ever.

Book design by Sylvia Frezzolini Severance
New Directions books are printed on acid-free paper.
Manufactured in the United States of America
First published clothbound by New Directions in 2003
Published simultaneously by Penguin Books Canada Limited

Library of Congress Cataloging-in-Publication Data

The New Directions anthology of classical Chinese poetry / edited by
    Eliot Weinberger; translations by William Carlos Williams . . . [et al.].
        p. cm.
    Includes bibliographical references.
        ISBN 0-8112-1605-5 (alk. paper)
    1. Chinese poetry—Translations into English. 2. Chinese
    poetry—History and criticism. I. Weinberger, Eliot. II. Williams,
    William Carlos, 1883–1963.
        PL2658.E3N46 2003
                            2002156731

New Directions Books are published for James Laughlin
by New Directions Publishing Corporation,
80 Eighth Avenue, New York, NY 10011

SECOND PRINTING

CONTENTS

T'ANG POETS (618–907)

LI PO

SUNG POETS (960–1279)

ON CHINESE POETRY

HSIN: (From *hatchet, to erect*, and *wood*.) To cut down wood; fresh; new; to renovate; to renew or improve the state of; to restore or to increase what is good, —applied to persons increasing in virtue; and to the daily increase of plants.

hsin¹

JIH: (Intended to represent the object.) The sun; the day; a day; daily; every day.

—Rev. Robert Morrison,
A Dictionary of the Chinese Language, 1815-1823

jih⁴

They say that characters were engraven on the bathing tub of King Tching Thang to this effect: "Renew thyself completely each day; do it again, and again, and forever again." I can understand that. Morning brings back the heroic ages.

—Henry David Thoreau, *Walden*, 1854

jih⁴

Tching prayed on the mountain and
    wrote MAKE IT NEW
on his bath tub
    Day by day make it new

—Ezra Pound, Canto LIII, 1940

hsin¹

INTRODUCTION

Like the flapping kookaburra in Australia that sets off a tornado in Kansas, poetry operates under its own version of chaos theory: the unpredictable effects of remote, sometimes forgotten causes. A 4th-century poet from Gupta India, Kalidasa, becomes a founding father of German Romanticism; Buddhist Jataka tales turn up in Chaucer; a Finnish pseudo-folk epic sets the beat for the pseudo-folk epic called "Hiawatha"; an 11th-century Persian, Omar the Tentmaker (Khayyam) transfixes the Victorians. . . and, in the 20th century, American poetry is inextricable from classical Chinese poetry and the Chinese language itself.

In 1909, there had only been about a dozen English translations of Chinese poetry in 150 years, mainly obscure books done by diplomats and missionaries, and a poet like Li Po sounded like this (the translator is L. Cranmer-Byng):

> And now Spring beckons with verdant hand,
> And Nature's wealth of eloquence doth win
> Forth to the fragrant-bowered nectarine,
> Where my dear friends abide, a careless band.

The received wisdom, as articulated by Lytton Strachey the year before, was that Chinese poems

> are like odours, for all their intangibility, the strange compelling powers of suggested reminiscence and romance. Whatever their subject, they remain ethereal . . . perhaps the Western writer whose manner they suggest most constantly is Verlaine.

This was no surprise; in 1909, America's most innovative poet, Ezra Pound, was writing like this:

> Autumnal breaks the flame upon the sun-set herds.
> The sheep on Gilead as tawn hair gleam
> Neath Mithra's dower and his slow departing,
> While in the sky a thousand fleece of gold
> Bear, each his tribute, to the waning god.

Six years later, in 1915, here was Pound:

> For a moment she rested against me
> Like a swallow half blown to the wall

And here was Li Po, as translated by Pound:

> Desolate castle, the sky, the wide desert.
> There is no wall left to this village.
> Bones white with a thousand frosts,
> High heaps, covered with trees and grass;
> Who brought this to pass?

What had happened in the interval was Pound's invention of Imagism, formally launched in the March 1913 issue of *Poetry* as an assault on the reigning abstractions and rhetorical excesses, couched in predictable meters and rhymes. Its program was "direct treatment of the 'thing,'" without moralizing or commentary, a poetry where every word was essential and lines were organized according to musical phrases. After his revelation, in 1910, that "all ages are contemporaneous," Pound searched through the world's poetries for examples of Imagist principles, finding them in the Troubadours and in Dante, and even more concretely in the unreconstructed surviving lyrics of the *Palatine Anthology* and, in 1913, classical Chinese.

That year, Pound enthusiastically read the manuscript of *Scented Leaves— from a Chinese Jar*, invented "Chinese" prose poems by Allen Upward (1863–1926), a diplomat, politician, colonial judge in Nigeria, spy, erudite occultist, Irish nationalist, gossip columnist, pulp fiction writer, author of a 300-page letter to the Swedish Academy on the meaning of the word "idealist," and ultimate suicide. Pound declared that Upward was also an Imagist (Upward: "I had no idea what he meant.") and sent his poems on to *Poetry*.

Upward's leaves had been inspired by a reading of Herbert A. Giles' 1901 *History of Chinese Literature* (Upward: "I perceived that we in the West were indeed barbarians and foreign devils, and that we knew scarcely anything about poetry."), and he urged Pound to get the book. It was the first such history in English, a work of excellent scholarship, though of dreadful translations. Pound, remarkably—given what was known about Chinese poetry at the time—extracted four short poems from Giles' weed-choked verbiage [see the entries and notes to Ch'ü Yüan, Liu Ch'e, and Pan Chieh-yü for both versions]. Along with two other poems, they became his own contribution to the *Des Imagistes* anthology, which he edited, publishing it the following year.

Classical Chinese was thus already on the Imagist agenda when, in November of 1913, Pound received the Rosetta Stone of American modernism: the Fenollosa manuscripts. Ernest Fenollosa (1853–1908) had gone from Harvard to the University of Tokyo, as Japan was opening to the West, to teach philosophy and economics. There he amassed a vast art collection, sold it to the Boston Museum, and became its Curator of Oriental Art. He knew little Japanese and no Chinese. A keeper of notebooks rather than a writer of books, his two-volume study, *Epochs of Chinese and Japanese Art*, was assembled by his wife Mary after his death; though more impressionistic than scholarly, it remained a standard text for decades.

From 1896 to 1901, Fenollosa undertook a study of Japanese Noh plays and Chinese poetry under the guidance of a series of Japanese professors, accompanied by interpreters. They worked through 150 Chinese poems, character by character, with Fenollosa meticulously writing down the Japanese pronunciation and literal translation of each, followed by a translation of the line and occasional commentary. The first line of what was to become Pound's "The River-Merchant's Wife: A Letter" ("While my hair was still cut straight across my forehead") looked like this in the notebooks:

Sho	*hatsu*	*sho*	*fuku*	*gaku*
mistress	hair	first	cover	brow

Chinese lady's I or my beginning

My hair was at first covering my brows

                (Chinese method of wearing hair)

In her husband's belief that the "purpose of poetical translation is the poetry, not the verbal definitions in dictionaries," Mary Fenollosa almost psychically selected Pound, whom she barely knew, to do something with the notebooks, and gave him £40 for his time. A few weeks later, Pound left for Stone Cottage in Sussex, the first of three winter retreats with W. B. Yeats—Pound ostensibly serving as Yeats' secretary—working under the very trees that would be immortalized in *Winnie-the-Pooh*.

Pound turned first to the Noh plays, and his enthusiasm led Yeats to invent a kind of Irish Noh (most notably, *At the Hawk's Well*) which he would later describe in detail in his introduction to Pound's 1917 *'Noh,' or Accomplishment, A Study of the Classical Stage of Japan*. Sometime in 1914, Pound began work on the Chinese poems. (There are drafts, in various stages of completion, for many of the poems, but they have never been collected, and some of them are gathered here for the first time.) In 1915, he selected fourteen of them (later expanded to eighteen), added his translation of the contemporaneous Anglo-Saxon poem "The Seafarer"—partially to demonstrate that when English poetry was first forming, Chinese poetry was at its height—and published them as a pamphlet, *Cathay*.

The *Cathay* poems have become so acclimatized, seem so "normal"—if just slightly old-fashioned—in American poetic practice, that it is difficult to recuperate their impact. Pound had indeed become, in T. S. Eliot's famous line, "the inventor of Chinese poetry for our time," but this wasn't saying a great deal. (For "Chinese," substitute the word "Hungarian" or "Swahili.") More to the point was Ford Maddox Ford's comment about the poems: "What poetry should be, that they are." *Cathay* was the first great book in English of the new, plain-speaking, laconic, image-driven free verse. And more: that which was most modern was derived from poems more than a thousand years old. The new poetry was revealed as an eternal verity. Conversely, and proving Pound's point about the contemporaneity of all ages, that which was ancient was the most immediate: In the midst of the Great War, *Cathay* was a book of soldiers, border guards, ruined cities, abandoned wives, and friends saying goodbye. Pound's friend, the sculptor Henri Gaudier-Brzeska, writing from the trenches shortly before his death, said he read it aloud to the other soldiers to give them courage.

Yet *Cathay* is a book the Sinologists still love to hate. It was, after all, written by an American who knew no Chinese, working from the notes of an American who knew no Chinese, who was taking dictation from Japanese simultaneous interpreters who were translating the comments of Japanese professors. Fenollosa (or his interlocutors) made mistakes; Pound made mistakes reading Fenollosa's handwriting and was sometimes confused by the arrangement of the poems (notoriously, in one case, running two poems together as one). In the book, proper names weirdly appear in their Japanese pronunciations: among the poets, for example, Li Po is Rihaku, Wang Wei is Omakitsu, T'ao Ch'ien is To-Em-Mei. (Pound knew the Chinese names, but kept the Japanese versions perhaps to pay homage to Fenollosa's informants, perhaps to emphasize the idea of transmission from language to language and century to century.) And yet, scholars such as Wai-lim Yip have shown how Pound intuitively corrected errors in the notebooks. Many of the *Cathay* poems are presented here next to translations of the same poems by a reliable Sinologist, David Hinton. Readers may judge for themselves Pound's reputation for "infidelity," that watchword of translation's morality police.

Unexpectedly, it was not only Chinese poetry that spoke directly to the new age, but the perceived nature of the Chinese language itself. In 1914, early in the Fenollosa work, Pound was still thinking of poetry as a succession of clear and solid images. In an essay, he quotes a haiku (by, oddly, a Japanese naval officer):

> The foot-steps of the cat upon the snow:
> (are like) plum-blossoms.

commenting that he has added the words "are like" for clarity. (This is surprising, as he had already written "In a Station of the Metro," where "like" is replaced by a colon.) Sometime later, Pound read Fenollosa's draft of an essay, "The Chinese Written Character as a Medium for Poetry," and that copula, literally and metaphorically, would vanish from American modernism, and the image sequence would become a complex.

Fenollosa described how Chinese characters were "ideograms" composed of pictographic elements that combined to form a new word or concept. Thus the sun rising in the branches of a tree became "east." (In fact, this is true of only a small fraction of Chinese characters, which are largely phonetic, but the mistake was fruitful.) More than a still life of elements placed side by side, a word and its meaning were generated by the dynamic relations among the elements. Moreover, Chinese made no distinction between noun, verb, and adjective (again, only partially true), which meant that every ideogram was a node of energy—thing and action and its description—a configuration of elements that, in turn, became an element, without Western rhetorical glue, in the succession of characters in a line of poetry. Fenollosa saw this as a "moving picture" (as did, completely independently, Sergei Eisenstein, whose studies of Chinese led to his theory of montage and his 1929 essay, "The Cinematographic Principle and the Ideograph"). Pound saw it as a simultaneity. Here was modernism—Cubism, collage and assemblage, Apollinaire's "Zone"— recapitulated in every word of an ancient language. And here was something deeper: According to Fenollosa's Emersonian transcendentalist outlook, Chinese was "a vivid shorthand picture of the operations of nature" itself, which knows no pure verbs or nouns, things or actions in isolation, where everything is in active relation. (Henri Michaux would write: "Like nature, the Chinese language does not draw any conclusions of its own, but lets itself be read.") Chinese was the most natural language and therefore the most perfect for poetry.

For Pound, this ideogrammic way of both perceiving the world and creating art would ultimately radiate from the Chinese character itself (and his lifelong preoccupation with Chinese etymology, spurred on by the Rev. Robert Morrison's early 19th-century dictionary) to the making of the *Cantos*—individual ideograms composed of "radiant gists" of disparate elements, which in turn formed one, huge, unfinished ideogram—to Pound's whole life and work, a universe or metropolis of countless interacting, harmonious and contradictory things, writings, people, and ideas.

American poetry ever since can be divided into the linear (Frost, Stevens, later Eliot, Bishop, Lowell . . .) and the ideogrammic (early Eliot, Zukofsky, Oppen, Olson, Duncan . . .), but there is one more story to tell from those years. In 1913, a young Chinese student at Cornell, Hu Shih, read Pound's "A Few Don'ts by an Imagiste," applied it to the state of Chinese poetry (then still written in an attenuated literary language), and in 1917 published a manifesto, "Tentative Proposals for the Improvement of Literature," which later became known as the "Eight Don't-isms." Its clarion call for a new writing in the vernacular and a new literature for a new China flowed into the larger currents of the nationalistic, anti-imperial, and iconoclastic May Fourth Movement of 1919. Hu Shih found in America what Ezra Pound had found in China.

For a few years after *Cathay*, Pound translated more of the Fenollosa poems, but published no more Chinese poetry translations until the 1954 *Classic Anthology Defined by Confucius*, better known as *The Confucian Odes*. The Chinese corner of the Pound ideogram was preoccupied with translations of

Confucius—the *Ta Hio* in 1928, the *Analects* in 1937, two Italian versions in 1944 and 1945, *The Unwobbling Pivot & The Great Digest* in 1947—and *Cantos LII–LXXI* in 1940, a drastic condensation of the entirety of Père de Moyriac de Mailla's twelve-volume 18th-century *Histoire Générale de la Chine*, placed alongside the history of John Adams' America.

But *Cathay* had set off a small landslide of Chinese poetry translation. It was the fifteenth book in English since the era of Adams and de Mailla; in the next forty years there were at least another fifty—in a time of not many poetry books, and even fewer poetry translations—though most were unmemorable. Notable among them were, above all, the books of Arthur Waley, the first Sinologist capable of writing poetry, but one whose translations were often sunk by his fondness for Gerard Manley Hopkins and a theory that the number of stresses in the English line must match the number of characters in the Chinese. (In the end, Waley's greatest work may well be in prose and from the Japanese: *The Tale of Genji*.) Among the others, there was Amy Lowell, whose hostile takeover of Imagism—Pound quickly moved on to Vorticism—included a drippy 1921 collaboration with Florence Ayscough called *Fir-Flower Tablets* ("When the hair of your Unworthy One first began to cover her forehead"); and Witter Bynner and Kiang Kang-hu's *The Jade Mountain* (1929), important as the first English translation of the complete *300 Poems from the T'ang* anthology, and an inspiration for Kenneth Rexroth and Burton Watson, but written in ethereal mode, with many lines beginning or ending in ellipses.

The postwar period brought a second flowering of Chinese translation, and it began, again, with Pound, in 1946. Awaiting trial and possible execution for treason for his wartime radio broadcasts, he was locked in the ward (he called it the "hell-hole") for the criminally insane in St. Elizabeths Hospital in Washington, D.C., with few privileges and infrequent visitors. He preoccupied himself with a translation of the *Shih Ching*, the earliest Chinese anthology, for, as he would translate, "Only antient wisdom is / solace to man's miseries." A first draft was written, based only on James Legge's 1876 bilingual edition and Matthews' dictionary of modern usage. Later, when he was moved to a more benign section of the hospital, he had access to the work of the Swedish Sinologist Bernard Karlgren, some Chinese visitors, and a correspondence with the scholar Achilles Fang. The translation went through three completely different drafts before it was published in 1954.

The Confucian Odes was a very different book from *Cathay*. It was a complete text—all 305 poems of the original anthology—rather than a selection, which meant that Pound had to work through some dull stretches. It was an "ideogrammic" translation, in that Pound attempted to incorporate into the poems, along with the literal meanings, the etymological, pictographic elements of certain characters. [See the note to "Pine boat a-shift" for examples of this procedure.] Also ideogrammically, he inserted the poems into the simultaneity of all ages by frequently giving them wacky, culturally and historically specific titles like "Polonius on Ostentation," "Evviva la Torre di Pisa!," "Strip-Tease?," and "Ole Man River."

Most of all, Pound had become interested in the music of Chinese poetry. By the time *The Chinese Written Character* was first published in book form in 1936, Pound was already moving away from Fenollosa's purely visual reading. In some new notes to the text, he emphasized the "verbal sonority" of Chinese ("I now doubt if it was inferior to the Greek") and, moreover, that the poems must be sung. In the insane asylum, Pound carefully transcribed the sounds of each line of the *Odes*, mixing modern usage with Karlgren's reconstructions of the archaic pronunciations, and he practiced chanting them. (The original edition was supposed to include the Chinese text and these transliterations, but the publisher, Harvard University Press, objected to the expense.) The entire book was conceived as a songbook, with Pound's oceanic eclecticism finding models from the Troubadours to the Elizabethans, hillbilly folk songs to some syncopated boogie-woogie. Rarely discussed by Pound scholars and completely dismissed by Sinologists, *The Confucian Odes* remains—alongside Samuel Beckett's anthology of Mexican poetry and Louis Zukofsky's Catullus—one of the masterpieces of idiosyncratic translation: a radical invocation of the spirits, if not always an accurate transmission of the words.

In 1947, Robert Payne had a poetry bestseller with *The White Pony*, the first anthology to survey the entirety of Chinese poetry, from the *Shih Ching* to the still renegade Mao Zedong. In 1956, Kenneth Rexroth had another bestseller with his *One Hundred Poems from the Chinese*. Thirty-five of the hundred poems were by Tu Fu ("without question the major influence on my own poetry"), who at the time was still eclipsed in English by Pound's Li Po and Waley's Po Chü-i; the rest were the first important translations of various Sung Dynasty poets, who had generally been neglected in the prevailing T'angophilia. Rexroth, in his unreliable *An Autobiographical Novel*, claimed that he first began learning Chinese as a boy; in 1924, at nineteen, he met Witter Bynner in Taos, who spurred his interest in Tu Fu. According to his introduction to *One Hundred*, the poems were derived from the Chinese texts, as well as French, German, and academic English translations, but the sources hardly matter. Rexroth had reimagined the poems as the work of someone on the other side of the Pacific Rim, speaking in a plain, natural-breathing, neutral American idiom. Ignoring the Chinese line, which is normally a complete syntactical unit, Rexroth enjambed his, often with end-stops in the middle, to give them the illusion of effortless speech. *One Hundred* was followed in 1970 by *Love and the Turning Year: One Hundred More Poems from the Chinese*, possibly his best translation, a selection of favorite poems from two thousand years of poetry.

More than any other translator of Chinese, it is almost impossible to separate Rexroth's translations from his own poetry; they tend to speak as one. And in the 1970s, his Chinese (and Japanese) translations became part of a strange project in old age to reinvent himself as a woman poet. Along with his creation of a young Japanese poet, Marichiko, and her erotic lyrics, and an anthology of Japanese women poets, Rexroth collaborated with the scholar Ling Chung on *The Orchid Boat: Women Poets of China* (1972) and, two years later, an edition of the complete poems of the great Sung poet, Li Ch'ing Chao. Like Whitman, Rexroth was containing multitudes, but they were all East Asian women.

Among the things in Chinese poetry that directly appealed to Rexroth and Gary Snyder (and later David Hinton) was its celebration of wilderness—something that had been neglected by Pound and Waley, Lowell and Bynner. Many Chinese poets, whether in exile or in Taoist or Buddhist retreat, had inhabited landscapes as dramatic and wild as those of the American West, and the poems they wrote had no equivalent in world literature, where nature tended to be domesticated or fearsome. In the notes here, Snyder tells how his work in the national forests informed his early studies of Chinese poetry; both he and Rexroth, because of their extensive wilderness experience—and a Buddhist training to place it in context—were able to see the natural specifics of Chinese poetry in a way that more desk-bound translators were not.

Snyder's Chinese studies began in the late 1940s, and he has said that, if it weren't for the Chinese revolution and its hostility both to Westerners and Buddhists, the path that led him to spend years in Japan probably would have taken him to China. Although he hasn't translated a great deal, his Han Shan poems, first published in 1958, are a colloquial classic ("Try to make it to Cold Mountain") that transformed a semi-legendary Buddhist itinerant monk into an American Beat. Sometime in the late 1970s, Snyder started working on *The Great Clod*, an unfinished eco-cultural history of China, sections of which are included here, and he has occasionally translated other poems since, though unfortunately very few.

In 1957, William Carlos Williams at age 74 began to translate Chinese poetry, in collaboration with the exceedingly bizarre David Rafael Wang (1931–1977). Wang, also known as David Happell Hsin-fu Wand, was born in China—a direct descendant, he claimed, of Wang Wei—escaped to the U. S. after the revolution, and became surely the only Chinese-American who was both a pseudo-Nazi white supremacist (and a member of the seedier circles around Pound in St. Elizabeths) and a Black Panther (in Oakland in the 1960s). Among other things, he was also a stodgy professor, active in the academic bureaucracy; a bisexual martial arts fanatic; a poet ("in the Greco-Sino-Samurai-African tradition") and friend of many of the Beat and Black Mountain poets, who had long talks about poetry with Muhammad Ali; a translator of Hawaiian and Samoan oral poetries, included in the Rothenberg *Technicians of the Sacred* anthology; and a possible suicide (at a MLA convention) who some people believe was murdered. Williams, however, apparently kept the conversation to Chinese poetry, and their four-year collaboration resulted in "The Cassia Tree," a group of 37 poems, published in 1966, after Williams' death.

Cathay had led Williams to Giles' *History*, and references to China and Chinese poetry appear as early as *Kora in Hell* (1918). In his library were most of the major translations of poetry and prose, and it is quite possible that the progressively thinner poems he began writing in 1917 were inspired by a book he owned called *Chinese Made Easy* (1904), which included the text and a translation of the pedagogical *Three Character Classic* running down the page. That the strict formal qualities of Chinese poetry would also have their effect on American poetry is unexpected but true: Louis Zukofsky, for one, following the Chinese, wrote passages of *"A"* using the number of words, not syllables or stresses, as the unit of measure.

Along with the poets, the postwar period was also a time of excellent translations by Sinologists: among them, A. C. Graham and David Hawkes in the U. K., and J. P. Seaton and Jonathan Chaves in the U. S. Rare among foreign-language experts, they were readers of contemporary English-language poetry, and they not only knew where the poems were coming from, but where they were going. Unquestionably the greatest of all has been Burton Watson. His many books of poetry translation (along with classics of philosophy and Buddhism, and his own critical studies) are written in a modest, plain-speaking English whose perfection becomes apparent as soon as they are compared with other translations.

David Hinton represents a new generation in this tradition. A prolific scholar-translator, in a dozen years he has already produced book-length selections of six classic poets, two books of the contemporary poet Bei Dao, an anthology of wilderness poetry, and translations of the four major philosophers. His poetry versions are a new chapter in the history of Chinese translation. Against the reigning style—forged by Rexroth, Snyder, and Watson—which assumes that the Chinese direct apprehension of the real world must be presented in direct, conversational speech, Hinton has attempted to recreate some of the density of classical Chinese, without resorting, as some others have done, to a pidgin English. A Hinton translation, like a Chinese poem, tends to reveal itself slowly, with several readings.

How classical Chinese entered into American poetry is a simple story, but its effect may never be fully unraveled, for it is often impossible to determine whether the Americans found in it a revelation or merely a confirmation of what they had already discovered.

In the Imagist aesthetic, which has dominated American poetry for the last ninety years, Chinese was perhaps the greatest example of direct presentation without generalizing comment, of "no ideas except in things." Poets as dissimilar as Charles Reznikoff and Stanley Kunitz, to take one example, each publicly cited the Sung Dynasty critic, Wei T'ai (from the epigraph to A. C. Graham's *Poems of the Late T'ang*): "Poetry presents the thing in order to convey the feeling. It should be precise about the thing and reticent about the feeling."

In the modernist project of a poetry that would be about everything, that was open to anything, even (or especially) the most ordinary experiences, Chinese was a poetry where Tu Fu could begin a poem with the crumbling of the state and end complaining that he's gone bald. It was a poetry that made no distinctions about what was suitable for poetry, and one where it was already assumed that so much depended upon a red wheelbarrow.

As the postwar poets moved into the American wilderness, they found that Chinese poetry, created in a similarly vast landscape, slaked (in Gary Snyder's words) "the modern thirst for natural, secular clarity" for it

> seems to have found, at its finest, a center within the poles of man, spirit & nature. With strategies of apparent simplicity and understatement it moves us from awe before history, to a deep breath before nature, to a laugh before spirit.

For those who believed, like Pound, that a wise government consults its poets, Chinese was a poetry largely written by civil servants with varying degrees of political power, and sometimes by the emperors themselves. For those like Snyder and Rexroth in Cold War America, who believed in poetry as opposition to the State, the Chinese poet's role as the exiled or self-exiled recluse-sage in the wilderness was a model—and one, as Snyder has pointed out, not dependent, as is usual among Western oppositional figures, on an alternate theology or political ideology.

In the daily assault of mendacious or empty language, Chinese poetry promoted the Confucian "rectification of names"—that words should mean what they say, that it is the poet's task to restore meaning, that the poet, like the enlightened ruler, was a person who stood by his word. In the new morality, the eroticism of Chinese lyrics was unabashed, polymorphous, and just plain sexy. In the age of cinematic montage, Chinese poetry leapt from word to word, line to line, and let the reader supply the transitions. Particularly for those who could not read it, it seemed to be a kind of concrete poetry, just at the moment when American poets were preoccupied with the look of the poem on the page. Most of all, it was a poetry where one found the whole panorama of enduring human emotions and experiences, lofty and mundane: war and the weather, loneliness and politics, drunkenness and minor aches and pains, friendship, gardening, bird-watching, failure, river journeys, religious and sexual ecstasy, aging, poverty and riches, courtesans and generals, princes and children, street vendors and monks. Chinese poetry as a whole was a Balzacian human comedy from a distant place and time that ultimately didn't seem so remote at all.

This anthology partially illustrates American poetry's unlikely and fortuitous romance with Chinese through the work of the four major poets who translated Chinese and an important scholar-translator—all of them, not coincidentally, having long associations with New Directions, the primary American publisher of international modernism. It is intended to be a book of poetry that may be read cover to cover; it is not a reference work. (The dream of comprehensiveness among anthologists and reviewers—a dream of a library, not a book—leads only to shelves of the massive and the unread.) As such, it necessarily has evident gaps: among the Chinese poets, simply because these translators never worked on them, and among those who have translated Chinese into English. Nevertheless, the hope is that it will serve as a collection of poems worth reading, as an introductory survey of classical Chinese poetry and a celebration of it by American poets, as a collage of commentaries by the American poets on the Chinese and by the Chinese poets on each other, and as a look at the process of translation itself through the presentation of multiple versions of the same poems, including some cases where the translators rewrote themselves.

Special thanks to David Hinton and Gary Snyder, to Peter Glassgold and Peggy Fox, and to Richard Sieburth, Ken Knabb, and Jeffrey Yang for information on, respectively, Pound, Rexroth, and Achilles Fang.

ELIOT WEINBERGER

EARLY POETS

(TO 618)

(I)

SONG OF THE BOWMEN OF SHU

Here we are, picking the first fern-shoots
And saying: When shall we get back to our country?
Here we are because we have the Ken-nin for our foemen,
We have no comfort because of these Mongols.
We grub the soft fern-shoots,
When anyone says "Return," the others are full of sorrow.
Sorrowful minds, sorrow is strong, we are hungry and thirsty.
Our defence is not yet made sure, no one can let his friend return.
We grub the old fern-stalks.
We say: Will we be let to go back in October?
There is no ease in royal affairs, we have no comfort.
Our sorrow is bitter, but we would not return to our country.
What flower has come into blossom?
Whose chariot? The General's.
Horses, his horses even, are tired. They were strong.
We have no rest, three battles a month.
By heaven, his horses are tired.
The generals are on them, the soldiers are by them.
The horses are well trained, the generals have ivory arrows and
      quivers ornamented with fish-skin.
The enemy is swift, we must be careful.
When we set out, the willows were drooping with spring,
We come back in the snow,
We go slowly, we are hungry and thirsty,
Our mind is full of sorrow, who will know of our grief?

[EP, 1915]

Pick a fern, pick a fern, ferns are high,
"Home," I'll say: home, the year's gone by,
no house, no roof, these huns on the hoof.
Work, work, work, that's how it runs,
We are here because of these huns.

Pick a fern, pick a fern, soft as they come,
I'll say "Home."
Hungry all of us, thirsty here,
no home news for nearly a year.

Pick a fern, pick a fern, if they scratch,
I'll say "Home," what's the catch?
I'll say "Go home," now October's come.
King wants us to give it all,
no rest, spring, summer, winter, fall,
Sorrow to us, sorrow to you.
We won't get out of here till we're through.

When it's cherry-time with you,
we'll see the captain's car go thru,
four big horses to pull that load.
That's what comes along our road,
What do you call three fights a month,
and won 'em all?

Four car-horses strong and tall
and the boss who can drive 'em all
as we slog along beside his car,
ivory bow-tips and shagreen case
to say nothing of what we face
sloggin' along in the Hien-yün war.

Willows were green when we set out,
it's blowin' an' snowin' as we go
down this road, muddy and slow,
hungry and thirsty and blue as doubt
(no one feels half of what we know).

[EP, 1954]

Pine boat a-shift
on drift of tide,
for flame in the ear, sleep riven,
driven; rift of the heart in dark
no wine will clear,
nor have I will to playe.

Mind that's no mirror to gulp down all's seen,
brothers I have, on whom I dare not lean,
angered to hear a fact, ready to scold.

My heart no turning-stone, mat to be rolled,
right being right, not whim nor matter of count,
true as a tree on mount.

Mob's hate, chance evils many, gone through,
aimed barbs not few;
at bite of the jest in heart
start up as to beat my breast.

O'ersoaring sun, moon malleable
alternately
lifting a-sky to wane;
sorrow about the heart like an unwashed shirt, I
clutch here at words,
having no force to fly.

[EP]

Locusts a-wing, multiply.
Thick be thy
posterity.

Locusts a-wing with heavy sound;
strong as great rope may thy line
abound.

Wing'd locust, that seem to cease,
in great companies hibernate,
So may thy line last and be great
in hidden ease.

[EP]

Pluck, pluck, pluck, the thick plantain;
pluck, pick, pluck, then pluck again.

Oh pick, pluck the thick plantain,
Here be seeds for sturdy men.

Pluck the leaf and fill the flap,
Skirts were made to hide the lap.

[EP]

Three stars, five stars rise over the hill
We came at sunset, as was his will.
One luck is not for all.

In Orion's hour, Pleiads small
Came with coverlets to the high hall.
Sun's up now
Time to go.
One luck is not for all.

[EP]

Lies a dead deer on younder plain
whom white grass covers,
A melancholy maid in spring
                              is luck
                              for
                              lovers.

Where the scrub elm skirts the wood,
be it not in white mat bound,
as a jewel flawless found,
                 dead as doe is maidenhood.

Hark!
Unhand my girdle-knot,
                 stay, stay, stay
                 or the dog
                 may
                 bark.

                                        [EP]

Lily bud floating, yellow as sorrow,
grief today, what of tomorrow?

Gone the bud, green the leaf,
better unborn than know my grief.

Scrawny ewes with swollen heads,
the fish traps catch but stars.

What man has food now
after these many wars?

                                        [EP]

Withered, withered, by the wind's omen,
a state lost for the soft mouth of a woman;

What the wind hath blown away,
can men of Cheng rebuild it in a day.

[EP]

Wide, Ho?
A reed will cross its flow;
Sung far?
One sees it, tip-toe.

Ho strong?
The blade of a row-boat cuts it so soon.
Sung far? I could be there
(save reverence) by noon
      (did I not venerate
      Sung's line and state.)

[EP]

Don't chop that pear tree,
Don't spoil that shade;

Thaar's where ole Marse Shao used to sit,
Lord, how I wish he was judgin' yet.

[EP]

Heaven conserve thy course in quietness,
Solid thy unity, thy weal endless
that all the crops increase and nothing lack
in any common house.

Heaven susteyne thy course in quietness
that thou be just in all, and reap
so, as it were at ease, that every day
seem festival.

Heaven susteyne thy course in quietness
To abound and rise as mountain hill and range
constant as rivers flow that all augment
steady th' increase in ever cyclic change.

Pure be the victuals of thy sacrifice
throughout the year as autumns move to springs,
above the fane to hear "ten thousand years"
spoke by the manes of foregone dukes and kings.

Spirits of air assign felicity:
thy folk be honest, in food and drink delight;
dark-haired the hundred tribes concord
in act born of thy true insight.

As moon constant in phase; as sun to rise;
as the south-hills nor crumble nor decline;
as pine and cypress evergreen the year
be thy continuing line.

[EP]

1
Soft wind of the vale
that brings the turning rain,
          peril, foreboding;
Come time of quiet and revelry
you'll cast me from your company.

2
Idle the valley wind, hot tempest then,
far in your pleasure, near in your pain.
Came time of quiet revelry
You cast me from your company.

3
Scorching breath on the height, grief,
all grass must die, no tree but loseth leaf
Soft is the valley wind, harsh on the crest,
You remember the worst of me
Forgetting the best.

[EP]

How cut haft for an axe?

Who hacks
holds a haft.
To take a wife
properly
one gets a notary.

To hack an axe-haft
an axe
hacks;
the pattern's near.

Let who weds never pass
too far
from his own class.

[EP]

(Fluid as water that all tones reflects
of ten-day passion that no man respects.)

Under the hill to stand
tapping a hand-drum, waving an egret's feather,

Tapping an earthen pot on Yüan Road,
winter or summer, man
you weigh as much as your load:
                              the egret fan.

[EP]

A boat floats over shadow, two boys were aboard.
There is a cloud over my thought
and of them no word.

The boat floats past the sky's edge, lank sail a-flap;
and a dark thought inside me: how had they hap?

[EP]

Made his hut in the vale, a tall man stretched out
sleeps, wakes and says: no room for doubt.

Lean-to on torrent's brink, laughter in idleness,
sleeps, wakes and sings; I will move less.

In a hut on a butte, himself his pivot, sleeps,
wakes, sleeps again,
swearing he will not communicate
with other men.

[EP]

By curvèd bank
in South Mount's innerest wood
clamped as the bamboo root, rugged as pine,
let no plots undermine
this brotherhood.

Heir'd to maintain the lines
carnal and uterine;
doors west and south,
reared up the mile-long house
wherein at rest to dwell,
converse and jest.

Tight bound the moulds wherein to ram down clay,
beaten the earth and lime gainst rain and rat,
no wind shall pierce to cold the Marquis' state
nor bird nest out of place,
here is he eaved,
who moves as on winged feet,
sleeves neat
as a pheasant's wing,
prompt as the arrow's point
to the bull's-eye.
And here the audience hall,

Rich court in peristyle
with columns high
their capitals contrived right cunningly;
cheery the main parts,
ample the recess
where he may have repose in quietness.

Mat over mat, bamboo on rush
so it be soft, to sleep, to wake in hush,
from dreams of bears and snakes?
                Saith the diviner:

Which mean
Bears be for boys; snakes, girls.
Boys shall have beds, hold sceptres for their toys,
creep on red leather,
bellow when they would cry
in embroidered coats
ere come to Empery.

Small girls shall sleep on floor and play with tiles,
wear simple clothes and do no act amiss,
cook, brew and seemly speak,
conducing so the family's quietness.

[EP]

Cleared by its flowing, dip the flood water up
and it will steam thy rice or other
grain; a deferent prince is
to his people both father and mother.

Rain-water cleared by its overflood
if thou ladle it out will wash thy altar jar;
To a fraternal prince will his folk
return, as to home from afar.

In a fraternal prince his folk have rest,
as from rain water
cleared by its flowing thou hast
a pure house, or thy garden is blest.

[EP]

Great hand King Wu
vied not, made heat.
He drew not as sun
rest from work done.

Shang- Ti (over sky)
king'd our Ch'eng and K'ang;
bound all four coigns;
hacked clear their light.

Gong, drum, sound out,
stone, flute, clear in tone
ring in strong grain;
bring here hard ears.

Work, true, shall pay.
As we've drunk we are full,
Luck ev-er is and shall
Come with new grain.

[EP]

Green robe, green robe, lined with yellow,
Who shall come to the end of sorrow?

Green silk coat and yellow skirt,
How forget all my heart-hurt?

Green the silk is, you who dyed it;
Antient measure, now divide it?

Nor fine nor coarse cloth keep the wind
from the melancholy mind;
Only antient wisdom is
solace to man's miseries.

                                          [EP]

AFTER CH'U YUAN

I will get me to the wood
Where the gods walk garlanded in wistaria,
By the silver blue flood
    move others with ivory cars.
There come forth many maidens
    to gather grapes for the leopards, my friend,
For there are leopards drawing the cars.

I will walk in the glade,
I will come out from the new thicket
    and accost the procession of maidens.

[EP]

LIU CH'E

The rustling of the silk is discontinued,
Dust drifts over the court-yard,
There is no sound of foot-fall, and the leaves
Scurry into heaps and lie still,
And she the rejoicer of the heart is beneath them:

A wet leaf that clings to the threshold.

[EP]

AUTUMN WIND

The autumn wind blows white clouds
About the sky. Grass turns brown.
Leaves fall. Wild geese fly south.
The last flowers bloom, orchids
And chrysanthemums with their
Bitter perfume. I dream of
That beautiful face I can
Never forget. I go for
A trip on the river. The barge
Rides the current and dips with
The white capped waves. They play flutes
And drums, and the rowers sing.
I am happy for a moment
And then the old sorrow comes back.
I was young only a little while,
And now I am growing old.

[KR]

LAMENT OF A GRAYING WOMAN

White as the snow on mountaintop,
Bright as the moon piercing the clouds,
Knowing that you have a divided heart,
I come to you before you are gone.

We have lived long together in this town.
What need is there for a feast of wine?
But a feast we must have today,
For tomorrow we'll be by the stream
And I'll lag behind you at the fork,
Watching the waters flow east or west.

Tears and still more tears.
Why should we lament?
If only there is a constant man
Till white-hair shall we never part!

[WCW]

PAN CHIEH-YÜ (LADY PAN)

(I)
FAN-PIECE, FOR HER IMPERIAL LORD

O fan of white silk,
   clear as frost on the grass-blade,
You also are laid aside.

[EP]

(II)
A PRESENT FROM THE EMPEROR'S NEW CONCUBINE

I took a piece of the rare cloth of Ch'i,
White silk glowing and pure as frost on snow,
And made you a fan of harmony and joy,
As flawlessly round as the full moon.
Carry it always, nestled in your sleeve.
Wave it and it will make a cooling breeze.
I hope, that when Autumn comes back
And the North wind drives away the heat,
You will not store it away amongst old gifts
And forget it, long before it is worn out.

[KR]

A BALLAD OF THE MULBERRY ROAD

The sun rises in south east corner of things
To look on the tall house of the Shin
For they have a daughter named Rafu,
        (pretty girl)
She made the name for herself: "Gauze Veil,"
For she feeds mulberries to silkworms.
She gets them by the south wall of the town.
With green strings she makes the warp of her basket,
She makes the shoulder-straps of her basket
        from the boughs of Katsura,
And she piles her hair up on the left side of her head-piece.

Her earrings are made of pearl,
Her underskirt is of green pattern-silk,
Her overskirt is the same silk dyed in purple,
And when men going by look on Rafu
        They set down their burdens,
They stand and twirl their moustaches.

                         [EP]

THE BEAUTIFUL TOILET

Blue, blue is the grass above the river
And the willows have overfilled the close garden.
And within, the mistress, in the midmost of her youth,
White, white of face, hesitates, passing the door.
Slender, she put forth a slender hand;

And she was a courtezan in the old days,
And she has married a sot,
Who now goes drunkenly out
And leaves her too much alone.

                         [EP]

(I)

She weaves and ends no pattern to day
                    Milky way girl
and the heavy ox pulls and pulls
to the end of the day no pattern
Via lactea clear and shallow
far from each other
                            one wide river to cross

                                                        [EP]

(II)

By the river of stars, its brightness
                    the ox herd far from stargirl
her white hand on the shuttle
                    and at day's end no pattern yet made

a rain of tears for their distance
                    tho' the river is clear and shallow
                    they cannot cross it;

nor their pulse beat, come into words.

                                                        [EP]

SHE THINKS OF HER BELOVED

It is going to rain.
The fresh
Breeze rustles the leaves of the
Cinnamon tree. It scatters
The begonias on the earth.
The falling petals cannot
Be numbered. Scarlet leaves fly
In the wind. The wind raises
Whirls of dust. All the world trembles.
It blows over the gauze screen,
Chills my flesh
And disarranges
My hair. Desolate and alone
I dream of my beloved
At the edge of Heaven, far
Across towering mountain
Ranges and roaring rivers.
I watch the birds wheel in the
Starry sky. I wish they could
Carry a letter. But he
Is too far away, they would
Never find the way. Rivers
Flow to the sea. Nothing can
Make the current return to
Its source. Lustrous and perfumed,
The magnolias lose their petals
All through the day and the night
I loosen the agate pegs
Of the lute and put the jade
Flute back in its case. In the
Silence and solitude, the sound
Of my beating heart frightens me.
The moon breaks through the clouds. I try
To write a poem in the endless night.

[KR]

T'AO CH'IEN

TO-EM-MEI'S "THE UNMOVING CLOUD"

'Wet springtime,' says To-Em-Mei,
'Wet spring in the garden.'

I

The clouds have gathered, and gathered,
    and the rain falls and falls,
The eight ply of the heavens
    are all folded into one darkness,
And the wide, flat road stretches out.
I stop in my room toward the East, quiet, quiet,
I pat my new cask of wine.
My friends are estranged, or far distant,
I bow my head and stand still.

II

Rain, rain, and the clouds have gathered,
The eight ply of the heavens are darkness,
The flat land is turned into river.
    "Wine, wine, here is wine!"
I drink by my eastern window.
I think of talking and man,
And no boat, no carriage, approaches.

III

The trees in my east-looking garden
    are bursting out with new twigs,
They try to stir new affection,
And men say the sun and moon keep on moving
    because they can't find a soft seat.
The birds flutter to rest in my tree,
    and I think I have heard them saying,
"It is not that there are no other men
But we like this fellow the best,
But however we long to speak
He can not know of our sorrow."

[EP]

I RETURN TO THE PLACE I WAS BORN

From my youth up I never liked the city.
I never forgot the mountains where I was born.
The world caught me and harnessed me.
And drove me through dust, thirty years away from home.
Migratory birds return to the same tree.
Fish find their way back to the pools where they were hatched.
I have been over the whole country,
And have come back at last to the garden of my childhood.
My farm is only ten acres.
The farm house has eight or nine rooms.
Elms and willows shade the back garden.
Peach trees stand by the front door.
The village is out of sight.
You can hear dogs bark in the alleys,
And cocks crow in the mulberry trees.
When you come through the gate into the court
You will find no dust or mess.
Peace and quiet live in every room.
I am content to stay here the rest of my life.
At last I have found myself.

[KR]

(II)
HOME AGAIN AMONG GARDENS AND FIELDS

1
Nothing like the others, even as a child,
rooted in a love for hills and mountains,

I fell into their net of dust, that one
departure a blunder lasting thirteen years.

But a tethered bird longs for its forest,
a pond fish its deep waters. So now, my

land out on the south edge cleared, I
nurture simplicity among gardens and fields,

home again. I've got nearly two acres here,
and four or five rooms in my thatch hut.

Elms and willows shade the eaves out back,
and in front, peach and plum spread wide.

Distant—village people lost in distant
haze, kitchen smoke hangs above wide-open

country. Here, dogs bark deep in back roads,
and roosters crow from mulberry treetops.

No confusion within the gate, no dust,
my empty home harbors idleness to spare.

Back again: after so long in that trap,
I've returned to all that comes of itself.

2
So little out here ever involves people.
Visitors to our meager lane rare, my

bramble gate closed all day, this empty
home cuts dust-filled thoughts short.

And day after day, coming and going
on overgrown paths, I meet neighbors

without confusion: we only talk about
how the crops are doing, nothing more.

Mine grow taller each day, and my fields
grow larger, but I can't stop worrying:

come frost or sleet, and it all falls
into tatters, like so much tangled brush.

3
I planted beans below South Mountain.
A few sprouted, then brush took over.

I get up early to clear weeds, and
shouldering my hoe, return by moonlight.

The path narrow, the brush and trees
thick, evening dew pierces my clothes.

But they're not wet—just damp
enough it reminds me never to resist.

4
Years never wandering mountains and lakes
gone, elated again amid forests and fields,

I take children by the hand and set out
through woods and abandoned farmlands.

Soon, we're walking around aimlessly among
gravemounds and houses deserted long ago,

their wells and brick stoves still standing
here among broken-down bamboo and mulberry.

Someone is gathering firewood, so I ask
where these people are, all these people.

Turning toward me, he replies *Once you're
dead and gone, nothing's left.* They say

a single generation and, court or market,
every face is new. It's true, of course.

Life is its own mirage of change. It ends
vanished, returned into nothing. What else?

[DH]

from DRINKING WINE

3
I live in town without all that racket
horses and carts stir up, and you wonder

how that could be. Wherever the mind
dwells apart is itself a distant place.

Picking chrysanthemums at my east fence,
far off, I see South Mountain: mountain

air lovely at dusk, birds in flight
returning home. All this means something,

something absolute. Whenever I start
explaining it, I've forgotten the words.

[DH]

During the T'ai-yüan years [376–397 A.D.] of the Chin Dynasty, there was a man in Wu-ling who caught fish for a living. One day he went up a stream, and soon didn't know how far he'd gone. Suddenly, he came upon a peach orchard in full bloom. For hundreds of feet, there was nothing but peach trees crowding in over the banks. And in the confusion of fallen petals, there were lovely, scented flowers. The fisherman was amazed. Wanting to see how far the orchard went, he continued on.

The trees ended at the foot of a mountain, where a spring fed the stream from a small cave. It seemed as if there might be a light inside, so the fisherman left his boat and stepped in. At first, the cave was so narrow he could barely squeeze through. But he kept going and, after a few dozen feet, it opened out into broad daylight. There, on a plain stretching away, austere houses were graced with fine fields and lovely ponds. Dikes and paths crossed here and there among mulberries and bamboo. Roosters and dogs called back and forth. Coming and going in the midst of all this, there were men and women tending the fields. Their clothes were just like those worn by the people outside. And whether they were old with white hair or children in pigtails, they were all happy and of themselves content.

When they saw the fisherman, they were terribly surprised and asked where he had come from. Once he had answered all their questions, they insisted on taking him back home. And soon, they had set out wine and killed chickens for dinner. When the others in the village heard about this man, they all came to ask about him. They told him how, long ago, to escape those years of turmoil during the Ch'in Dynasty [221–207 B.C.], the village ancestors gathered their wives and children, and with their neighbors came to this distant place. And never leaving, they'd kept themselves cut-off from the people outside ever since. So now they wondered what dynasty it was. They'd never heard of the Han, let alone Wei or Chin. As the fisherman carefully told them everything he knew, they all sighed in sad amazement. Soon, each of the village families had invited him to their house, where they also served wine and food.

After staying for some days, the fisherman prepared to leave these people. As he was going, they said *There's no need to tell the people outside.* He returned to his boat and started back, careful to remember each place along the way.

When he got back home, he went to tell the prefect what had happened, and the prefect sent some men to retrace the route with him. They tried to follow the landmarks he remembered, but they were soon lost and finally gave up the search.

Liu Tzu-chi, who lived in Nan-yang, was a recluse of great honor and esteem. When he heard about this place, he joyfully prepared to go there. But before he could, he got sick and passed away. Since then, no one's asked the Way.

Ch'in's First Emperor ravaged the sense
heaven gives things, and wise people fled.

Huang and Ch'i left for Shang Mountain,
and these villagers were also never seen

again. Covering all trace of their flight,
the path they came on slowly grew over and

vanished. They worked hard tending fields
together, and come dusk, they all rested.

When mulberry and bamboo shade thickened,
planting time for beans and millet came.

Spring brought the silkworm's long thread,
and autumn harvests without taxes. There,

overgrown paths crossing back and forth,
roosters calling to the bark of dogs,

people used old-style bowls for ritual
and wore clothes long out of fashion. Kids

wandered at ease, singing. Old-timers
happily went around visiting friends.

Things coming into blossom promised mild
summer days, and bare trees sharp winds.

Without calendars to keep track, earth's
four seasons of themselves became years,

and happy, more than content, no one
worried over highbrow insights. A marvel

hidden away five hundred years, this
charmed land was discovered one morning,

but pure and impure spring from different
realms, so it soon returned to solitude.

Wandering in the world, who can fathom
what lies beyond its clamor and dust. O,

how I long to rise into thin air and
ride the wind in search of my own kind.

[DH]

ELEGY FOR MYSELF

It's the late-autumn pitch-tone *Wu-yi, Ting* year of the hare. The heavens are cold now, and the nights long. Geese pass, traveling south in desolate, windswept skies. Leaves turn yellow and fall. I, Master T'ao, will soon leave this inn awaiting travelers, and return forever to my native home. Everyone grieves. Mourning together, they've gathered here tonight for these farewell rites. They're making offerings to me: elegant foods and libations of crystalline wine. I look into their already blurred faces, listen to their voices blending away into silence.

Hu-ooo! Ai-tsai hu-ooo!

> Boundless—this vast heap earth,
> this bottomless heaven, how perfectly
>
> boundless. And among ten thousand
> things born of them, to find myself
>
> a person somehow, though a person
> fated from the beginning to poverty
>
> alone, to those empty cups and bowls,
> against winter cold.
>
> Even hauling water brought such joy,
> and I sang under a load of firewood:
>
> this life in brushwood-gate seclusion
> kept my days and nights utterly full.
>
> Spring and autumn following each other
> away, there was always garden work—
>
> some weeding here or hoeing there.
> What I tended I harvested in plenty,
>
> and to the pleasure of books, *koto*
> strings added harmony and balance.

I'd sun in winter to keep warm,
and summers, bathe in cool streams.

Never working more than hard enough,
I kept my heart at ease always,

and whatever came, I rejoiced in all
heaven made of my hundred-year life.

Nothing more than this hundred-year
life—and still, people resent it.

Afraid they'll never make it big,
hoarding seasons, they clutch at

days, aching to be treasured alive
and long remembered in death. Alone,

alone and nothing like them, I've
always gone my own way. All their

esteem couldn't bring me honor, so
how can mud turn me black? Resolute

here in my little tumbledown house,
I swilled wine and scribbled poems.

Seeing what fate brings, our destiny
clear, who can live without concern?

But today, facing this final change,
I can't find anything to resent:

I lived a life long and, cherishing
solitude always, abundant. Now

old age draws to a close, what more
could I want? Hot and cold pass

away and away. And absence returns,
something utterly unlike presence.

My wife's family came this morning,
and friends hurried over tonight.

They'll take me out into the country,
bury me where the spirit can rest

easy. O dark journey. O desolate
grave, gate opening into the dark

unknown. An opulent coffin Huan's
disgrace, Yang's naked burial a joke,

it's empty—there's nothing in death
but the empty sorrows of distance.

Build no gravemound, plant no trees—
just let the days and months pass

away. I avoided it my whole life,
so why invite songs of praise now?

Life is deep trouble. And death,
why should death be anything less?

   Hu-ooo! Ai-tsai hu-ooo!

[DH]

3

Boundless—in the boundless, weed-ridden
wastes, white poplars moan in the wind.

In bitter ninth-month frost, come to this
distant place—it's farewell. All four directions

empty, not a house in sight, looming
gravemounds peak and summit. Wind

moaning to itself in the branches here,
horses rear up, crying out toward heaven.

Once this dark house is all closed up,
day won't dawn again in a thousand years.

Day won't dawn again in a thousand years,
and what can all our wisdom do about it?

Those who were just here saying farewell
return to their separate homes. And though

my family may still grieve, the others
must be singing again by now. Once you're

dead and gone, what then? Trust yourself
to the mountainside. It will take you in.

[DH]

HSIEH LING-YÜN

from DWELLING IN THE MOUNTAINS

6
Here where I live,
lakes on the left, rivers on the right,
you leave islands, follow shores back

to mountains out front, ridges behind.
Looming east and toppling aside west,

they harbor ebb and flow of breath,
arch across and snake beyond, devious

churning and roiling into distances,
clifftop ridgelines hewn flat and true.

7
Nearby in the east are
Risen-Fieldland and Downcast-Lake,
Western-Gorge and Southern-Valley,

Stone-Plowshares and Stone-Rapids,
Forlorn-Millstone and Yellow-Bamboo.

There are waters tumbling a thousand feet in flight
and forests curtained high over countless canyons,

endless streams flowing far away into distant rivers
and cascades branching deeper into nearby creeks.

8
Nearby in the south are
two streams flowing together into a single
meander past three islands, all sincerity

doubled around inside out and outside in,
cleaving and fusing rivers and mountains.

Cliffs and pinnacles topple into flight on the east ridge,
curtained across to the west road, above rock-domed

islands where billows fill forests, and swelling waves
sweep white sand together and send water flowing away.

9
Nearby in the west are
Aspen and Guest Peaks sharing a mountain,
Halcyon and Emperor along a lazy ridgeline,

Stone-House Mountain facing Stone-Screen Cliff
across a gorge carved below Tier and Orphan,

its riverbanks thick bamboo coloring the current green,
reflected cliff-light turning mountain streamwater red.

Here the moon's hidden, darkened by peaks and summits,
and in rising wind, a forest of branches breaks into song.

10
Nearby in the north are
paired Shamaness Lakes linked together
and twin Lucent Streams threading ponds,

Perpetua Cliff split from Mount Athwart,
Compass and Blessing Peaks broken apart.

Embankments stretch on away, wandering along lakeshores,
and streams in flood cascading through gorges swell and surge

toward ponds and lakes that meander beneath towering cliffs.
There, among rocks churning with whitewater, the Way opens.

11
Far off to the east are
Tung-Cypress and Celestial-Terrace,
Stone-Window and Boundless-Peace,

Twin-Leeks and Fourfold-Radiance,
Fivefold-Shrine and Three-Reeds,

ranges and peaks all entered in books of divine marvels.
The rapport in things is tangible in the divine blessings

I wander among there, hiking Stone-Bridge's mossy trail
and beyond through the twisting gnarls of Oaken Gorge.

12
Far off to the south are
peaks like Pine-Needle and Nest-Hen,
Halcyon-Knoll and Brimmed-Stone,

Harrow and Spire Ridges faced together,
Elder and Eye-Loft cleaving summits.

When you go deep, following a winding river to its source,
you're soon bewildered, wandering a place beyond knowing:

cragged peaks towering above stay lost in confusions of mist,
and depths sunken away far below surge and swell in a blur.

13
Far off to the west are
        . . .

14

Far off to the north are
a long river flowing ever homeward
and the boundless seas taking it in.

Advent Ridge and sandbars wander away,
island mountains crowding together

below summits towering far and wide, sentinels watching over
waters meandering through depths and winding liquid away.

These wildlands, such wonder unceasing: they spread away into
wind-driven waves all struggle and repose together in the end.

15

It's emptiness to gaze along South Road's . . . . . .
. . . growing cliffs . . . become plateau . . .

. . . shorelines you can fathom the deep,
and seeing islands understand the shallow,

but when the water swells and billows full, rocks shelving up vanish,
and when the waves settle back clear again, sunken sand reappears.

Once rising winds start billows swelling,
water's power grows fierce and reckless,

and every year in spring and autumn,
the coming of new moons and full moons

startles waves into seething and churning
terror all surging and foundering deep.

Lightning swells and thunder tumbles,
torrents in flight and scattered cascades

brimming over impossible cliffs and rising into peaks
spread across midstream and gathering such distances,

swirling first in a flash and leaping out through the sky,
then toppling over into depths at last, revealing valleys.

A mere description of this realm was enough to cure a prince of Ch'u,
and meeting the Sea Lord here, even the River Spirit was overwhelmed.

18
Slipping from gardens to fields
and from fields on toward lakes,

I float and drift on and on along
rivers to realms of distant water,

sage pools in mountain streams deepening into recluse dark
and hazy confusions of wild rice clearing away along islands.

Fragrant springwater swells into springtime cascades here,
and chilled waves quicken amid autumn's passing clarity.

Wind churning up lakewater around islands full of orchids,
sunlight pours through pepper trees and on across the road,

and soaring lazily over the mid-stream island, the pavillion
there soaked in its luster, the moon in water is a perfect joy.

Lingering out shadows, mornings infuse things with clarity,
and suffusing the air, fragrant scents settle into evenings

here, where thinking of loved ones lost to me forever now,
I can look forward to the evanescent visits of cloud guests.

20
Many cures in *Essential Medicinals*
flourish among mountains and lakes.

Lords Thunder and Maple identified them,
Doctors Accord and Ease learned their uses:

the three seed-nuts and the six roots,
the five flowers and the nine fruits,

the two asparagus sharing a name but differing in nature
and three wolfsbane differing in form but found together,

water-scented orchids that flourish as autumn fades away,
forest orchids coming into lavish bloom when snows fly,

gnarled cypress that can outlive ten thousand dynasties,
and secretive china-root that's hidden a thousand years,

blossoms a radiant whorl of red petals gracing green stems,
leaves lush and silk-white drooping from purple branches.

They strengthen the spirit and make your life last and last,
dispel phantom demons, drive away malaise and affliction.

22
There are trees like
pine, cypress, sandalwood and oak,
· · · · · · , *wu-t'ung* and elm,

mulberries, rafterwood, stonethorn
and catalpas, tamarisk and ailanthus.

Ranging from steadfast to yielding
by nature, and from durable to frail,

they follow their own ways, rooted in
land high and low, fertile and barren:

trees you can't reach around keeping mountain peaks hidden,
their tops thousands of feet high parading through emptiness,

trees towering up in stately grandeur across ridgelines above
and spreading thick in shade along mountain streams below.

A tangle of hanging branches all through the long canyons,
they crowd together among rocks, making roads impossible

here, where blossoms reflected in water double their radiance
and *ch'i* wandering among them returns on the wind suffused,

where leek-green pines remain lovely through stark winters,
their fragrance growing lavish to welcome warmer weather:

they can bid farewell to autumn's tumble of scattering leaves
and wait out blossoms of springs till tucked inside their buds.

24
There are fish like
snake-fish and trout, perch and tench,
red-eye and yellow-gill, dace and carp,

bream, sturgeon, skate, mandarin-fish,
flying-fish, bass, mullet and wax-fish:

a rainbow confusion of colors blurred,
glistening brocade, cloud-fresh schools

nibbling duckweed, frolicking in waves,
drifting among ghost-eye, flowing deep.

Some drumming their gills and leaping through whitewater,
others beating their tails and struggling back beneath swells,

shad and salmon, each in their season, stream up into creeks and shallows,
sunfish and knife-fish follow rapids further, emerge in mountain springs.

25
There are birds like
junglefowl and swan, osprey, snow-goose,
crane and egret, bustard and kingfisher,

grouse and magpie like rich embroidery,
thrush and turkey like tasseled medallions,

ducks in dawn gatherings every morning,
pheasants at mountain bridges in season,

sea birds soaring in defiance of the wind,
and northern birds here fleeing the cold:

when buds open, they'll flock back north,
but frost-fall always sends them south again.

Greetings echo across Star River distances
as companions sleep along rivers and lakes:

if you listen to their crystalline calls here below, you can hear them
carrying Master Wang up through immortality skies and beyond,

and before long they're crossing back, returning on anxious wings
to the lavish pleasures that fill their days in these radiant valleys.

33
As for my
homes perched north and south,
inaccessible except across water:

gaze deep into wind and cloud
and you know this realm utterly.

34
At South Mountain,
three parks compassed by ridges
and two fields tight among canals,

nine springs swell into cascades,
five valleys to unearthly summits,

a confusion of ragged peaks towering up on all sides,
their slopes a throng of ascending knolls and shoulders,

and nearby, water floods down into surrounding fields,
following a tight network of dikes that stretches far-off,

far-off dikes connecting footpaths,
nearby streams opening cascades.

Crossing ridges and drifting waves
I go by water and return by foot,

return wandering and go roaming
winding isles and ringed pinnacles:

how could anything compare to this
joy and beauty so perfectly apparent?

I built my hut up here, facing northern summits,
its porch opening out onto vistas of southern peaks,

cliffs cragged up and spread away through the door,
an array of mirrored waves billowing at the window.

Taking cinnabar mist and haze for crimson lintels
and emerald clouds for kingfisher-green roofbeams,

I watch shooting stars streak down across the sky
and turn to gaze . . . . not yet out herding.

It isn't just swallows and sparrows that flutter short:
even soaring junglefowl and geese never make it

here, where a side spring surges
and tumbles down past the eastern eaves,

and between mighty opposing cliff-walls,
sounds of slipping rock fill the western eaves.

Tall bamboo stand in thick tangles of such delicate grace
and thickets of majestic trees deep in their lush seclusion:

vines spreading and spreading, climbing and wandering,
blossoms everywhere sweet fragrance and enticing beauty,

sun and moon cast their radiance over all these branches,
wind and dew opening utter clarity across forbidding peaks.

Summers cool and winters warm,
I abide by seasons, taking my ease

among winding stairs and terraces,
rafters and beams mounting apart.

My hut *ch'i*-sited among all this,
I delight in water and savor rock,

and watching things close at hand
year in and year out, I never tire,

though it hurts to see such beauty following change away.
Lamenting how we only borrow these drifting years of life,

I left the bustling crowds, vanishing into depths of solitude,
mind perennially given over to this rainbow life of clouds.

37
Rivers, mountains, streams, rocks,
islands, shores, wildflowers, trees:

you can attend to the singularity of things like that,
or you can weave them all into their place together:

Here where rivers flow crystal clear, no hint of mud,
and mountains are a blur of forests, never bare stone,

rocks lay strewn along forest edges up to jutting cliffs,
and freshets merge into streams, tumble down valleys

to deep water and meandering islands laced with scents.
Above shores all vagrant sand and bamboo reflection,

wildflowers greet winter with blossoms of frozen color,
and frost-covered trees flaunt their shivering green.

Facing northern shade
I find nestled snow against summer heat,
and facing southern sun
I find gentle warmth against winter cold.

Ridgelines here are
stacked up into systems of recluse summits,

and rising peaks are
crowded close and towering into lofty heights

where floating streams pour into flight, cascading through empty sky
toward swells surging up from the secret depths of mountain caverns.

All these things—
it's their singularity that makes them noble
together, each at ease in its own seasons.

47

In these remote and secluded depths of quiet mystery,
silence boundless, distances empty,

you see endeavor denies our nature
and appearance the inner pattern.

When eyes and ears can tell us nothing of such things,
how could anyone follow the path with mere footsteps?

I've distilled all antiquity in the steady cycle of seasons,
trusting to the enlightened insight of five-fold vision,

and now, abiding by this wisdom, I let my brush rest,
let shallow thoughts settle away and these words end.

[DH]

KILL THAT CROWING COCK

Kill that crowing cock.
Drive away the chattering birds.
Shoot the cawing crows.
I want this night to last
And morning never come back.
I don't want to see another dawn
For at least a year.

[KR]

THIS MORNING OUR BOAT LEFT

This morning our boat left the
Orchid bank and went out through
The tall reeds. Tonight we will
Anchor under mulberries
And elms. You and me, all day
Together, gathering rushes.
Now it is evening, and see,
We have gathered just one stalk.

[KR]

NIGHT WITHOUT END

Night without end. I cannot sleep.
The full moon blazes overhead.
Far off in the night I hear someone call.
Hopelessly I answer, "Yes."

[KR]

THE FISH WEEPS

The fish weeps in the
Dry riverbed. Too late he
Is sorry he flopped
Across the shallows. Now he
Wants to go back and
Warn all the other fishes.

[KR]

OUR LITTLE SISTER IS WORRIED

Our little sister is worried.
How long should she wait
To get married?
She has often seen the wind
Blow the peach petals from the trees.
She has never seen it
Blow them back on the branches.

[KR]

WHAT IS THE MATTER WITH ME?

What is the matter with me?
With all the men in the world,
Why can I think only of you?

[KR]

BITTER COLD

Bitter cold. No one is abroad.
I have been looking everywhere for you.
If you don't believe me,
Look at my footprints in the snow.

[KR]

1

We break off a branch of poplar catkins.
A hundred birds sing in the tree.
Lying beneath it in the garden,
We talk to each other,
Our tongues in each other's mouth.

2

The sultry air is heavy with flower perfumes.
What is there better to do this hot night
Than throw off the covers
And lie together naked?

3

A cold wind blows open the window.
The moon looks in, full and bright.
Not a sound,
Not a voice,
In the night.
Then from behind the bed curtains,
Two giggles.

4

A freezing sky.
The year ends.
Icy winds whirl the snowflakes.
Under the covers
My darling is hotter than midsummer night.

[KR]

T'ANG POETS

(618–907)

from COLD MOUNTAIN POEMS

The path to Han-shan's place is laughable,
A path, but no sign of cart or horse.
Converging gorges—hard to trace their twists
Jumbled cliffs—unbelievably rugged.
A thousand grasses bend with dew,
A hill of pines hums in the wind.
And now I've lost the shortcut home,
Body asking shadow, how do you keep up?

[GS]

In a tangle of cliffs I chose a place—
Bird-paths, but no trails for men.
What's beyond the yard?
White clouds clinging to vague rocks.
Now I've lived here—how many years—
Again and again, spring and winter pass.
Go tell families with silverware and cars
"What's the use of all that noise and money?"

[GS]

In the mountains it's cold.
Always been cold, not just this year.
Jagged scarps forever snowed in
Woods in the dark ravines spitting mist.
Grass is still sprouting at the end of June,
Leaves begin to fall in early August.
And here am I, high on mountains,
Peering and peering, but I can't even see the sky.

[GS]

Men ask the way to Cold Mountain
Cold Mountain: there's no through trail.
In summer, ice doesn't melt
The rising sun blurs in swirling fog.
How did I make it?
My heart's not the same as yours.
If your heart was like mine
You'd get it and be right here.

[GS]

I settled at Cold Mountain long ago,
Already it seems like years and years.
Freely drifting, I prowl the woods and streams
And linger watching things themselves.
Men don't get this far into the mountains,
White clouds gather and billow.
Thin grass does for a mattress,
The blue sky makes a good quilt.
Happy with a stone underhead
Let heaven and earth go about their changes.

[GS]

Clambering up the Cold Mountain path,
The Cold Mountain trail goes on and on:
The long gorge choked with scree and boulders,
The wide creek, the mist-blurred grass.
The moss is slippery, though there's been no rain
The pine sings, but there's no wind.
Who can leap the world's ties
And sit with me among the white clouds?

[GS]

Rough and dark—the Cold Mountain trail,
Sharp cobbles—the icy creek bank.
Yammering, chirping—always birds
Bleak, alone, not even a lone hiker.
Whip, whip—the wind slaps my face
Whirled and tumbled—snow piles on my back.
Morning after morning I don't see the sun
Year after year, not a sign of spring.

[GS]

In my first thirty years of life
I roamed hundreds and thousands of miles.
Walked by rivers through deep green grass
Entered cities of boiling red dust.
Tried drugs, but couldn't make Immortal;
Read books and wrote poems on history.
Today I'm back at Cold Mountain:
I'll sleep by the creek and purify my ears.

[GS]

I can't stand these bird-songs
Now I'll go rest in my straw shack.
The cherry flowers out scarlet
The willow shoots up feathery.
Morning sun drives over blue peaks
Bright clouds wash green ponds.
Who knows that I'm out of the dusty world
Climbing the southern slope of Cold Mountain?

[GS]

Cold Mountain has many hidden wonders,
People who climb here are always getting scared.
When the moon shines, water sparkles clear
When wind blows, grass swishes and rattles.
On the bare plum, flowers of snow
On the dead stump, leaves of mist.
At the touch of rain it all turns fresh and live
At the wrong season you can't ford the creeks.

[GS]

Cold Mountain is a house
Without beams or walls.
The six doors left and right are open
The hall is blue sky.
The rooms all vacant and vague
The east wall beats on the west wall
At the center nothing.

Borrowers don't bother me
In the cold I build a little fire
When I'm hungry I boil up some greens.
I've got no use for the kulak
With his big barn and pasture—
He just sets up a prison for himself.
Once in he can't get out.
Think it over—
You know it might happen to you.

[GS]

If I hide out at Cold Mountain
Living off mountain plants and berries—
All my lifetime, why worry?
One follows his karma through.
Days and months slip by like water,
Time is like sparks knocked off flint.
Go ahead and let the world change—
I'm happy to sit among these cliffs.

[GS]

I've lived at Cold Mountain—how many autumns.
Alone, I hum a song—utterly without regret.
Hungry, I eat one grain of Immortal-medicine
Mind solid and sharp; leaning on a stone.

[GS]

When men see Han-shan
They all say he's crazy
And not much to look at—
Dressed in rags and hides.
They don't get what I say
& I don't talk their language.
All I can say to those I meet:
"Try and make it to Cold Mountain."

[GS]

OLD IDEA OF CHOAN

I

The narrow streets cut into the wide highway at Choan,
Dark oxen, white horses,
    drag on the seven coaches with outriders.
The coaches are perfumed wood,
The jewelled chair is held up at the crossway,
Before the royal lodge:
A glitter of golden saddles, awaiting the princess;
They eddy before the gate of the barons.
The canopy embroidered with dragons
    drinks in and casts back the sun.
Evening comes.
    The trappings are bordered with mist.
The hundred cords of mist are spread through
    and double the trees,
Night birds, and night women,
Spread out their sounds through the gardens.

II

Birds with flowery wing, hovering butterflies
    crowd over the thousand gates,
Trees that glitter like jade,
    terraces tinged with silver,
The seed of a myriad hues,
A net-work of arbours and passages and covered ways,
Double towers, winged roofs,
    border the net-work of ways:
A place of felicitous meeting.

Riu's house stands out on the sky,
    with glitter of colour
As Butei of Kan had made the high golden lotus
    to gather his dews,
Before it another house which I do not know:
How shall we know all the friends
    whom we meet on strange roadways?

[EP]

(I)

Returning after I left my home in childhood,
I have kept my native accent but not the color of my hair.
Facing the smiling children who shyly approach me,
I am asked from where I come.

[WCW]

(II)

HOMECOMING

I was a boy when I left home.
I come back an old man.
I think I remember the country dialect,
But my hair has turned white since I spoke it.
Children stare at me.
Nobody understands me.
They look at me and laugh, and say,
"Where do you come from, Milord?"

[KR]

(I)

Steering my little boat towards a misty islet,
I watch the sun descend while my sorrows grow:
In the vast night the sky hangs lower than the treetops,
But in the blue lake the moon is coming close.

[WCW]

(II)

NIGHT ON THE GREAT RIVER

We anchor the boat alongside a hazy island.
As the sun sets I am overwhelmed with nostalgia.
The plain stretches away without limit.
The sky is just above the tree tops.
The river flows quietly by.
The moon comes down amongst men.

[KR]

(III)

MOORING ON CHIEN-TE RIVER

The boat rocks at anchor by the misty island
Sunset, my loneliness comes again.
In these vast wilds the sky arches down to the trees.
In the clear river water, the moon draws near.

[GS]

RETURNING BY NIGHT TO LU-MEN

I can hear the evening bell
In the mountain temple ringing
Above the voices of people
Calling for the ferry at
Fisherman's Crossing, and others
Going home to the village
Along the river beaches.
I take the boat back to Lu-Men.
On the mountain the moon shines
Through misty trees. At last I find
The ancient cabin of Lord P'ang,
Hidden by the cliffs,
On a path through the pines,
Where all is eternal peace,
And only a solitary
Man comes and goes by himself.

[KR]

(II)
RETURNING HOME TO DEER–GATE MOUNTAIN AT NIGHT

As day fades into dusk, the bell at a mountain temple sounds.
Fish-Bridge Island is loud with people clamoring at the ferry,

and others follow sandy shores toward their river village.
But returning home to Deer-Gate, I paddle my own little boat,

Deer-Gate's incandescent moonlight opening misty forests,
until suddenly I've entered old Master P'ang's isolate realm.

Cliffs the gate, pines the path—it's forever still and silent,
just this one recluse, this mystery coming and going of itself.

[DH]

(I)

In spring you sleep and never know when the morn comes,
    Everywhere you hear the songs of the birds,
But at night the sound of the wind mingles with the rain's,
    And you wonder how many flowers have fallen.

[WCW]

(II)
SPRING DAWN

Spring sleep, not yet awake to dawn,
I am full of birdsongs.
Throughout the night the sounds of wind and rain
Who knows   what flowers fell.

[GS]

LATE SPRING

In April the lake water is clear
Everywhere the birds are singing
The ground just swept, the petals fall again
The grass, though stepped on, remains green
My drinking companions gather to compare fortunes
Open the keg to get over the bout of drinking
With cups held high in our hands
We hear the voices of sing-song girls
ringing.

[WCW]

THE PEERLESS LADY

Look, there goes the young lady across the street
She looks about fifteen, doesn't she?
Her husband is riding the piebald horse
Her maids are scraping chopped fish from a gold plate.

Her picture gallery and red pavilion stand face to face
The willow and the peach trees shadow her eaves
Look, she's coming thru the gauze curtains to get into her chaise:
Her attendants have started winnowing the fans.

Her husband got rich early in his life
A more arrogant man you never find around!
She keeps busy by teaching her maids to dance
She never regrets giving jewels away.

There goes the light by her window screen
The green smoke's rising like petals on wave
The day is done and what does she do?
Her hair tied up, she watches the incense fade.

None but the bigwigs visit her house
Only the Chaos and the Lees get by her guards
But do you realize this pretty girl
Used to beat her clothes at the river's head?

[WCW]

Light rain is on the light dust.
The willows of the inn-yard
Will be going greener and greener,
But you, Sir, had better take wine ere your departure,
For you will have no friends about you
When you come to the gates of Go.

[EP]

DAWN ON THE MOUNTAIN

Peach flowers turn the dew crimson,
Green willows melt in the mist,
The servant will not sweep up the fallen petals,
        And the nightingales
Persist in their singing.

[EP]

Poor dwelling near valley mouth
High tree belts rough village
Palanquin twists about stone road
Who comes to gate of mountain abode?
Freezing bay glues fishing boat
Hunters fire burns in cold field
Only white cloud overhead
Temple bell and monkey cry rarely heard.

[EP]

Sitting in mystic bamboo grove, back unseen
Press stops of long whistle
Deep forest unpierced by man
Moon and I face each other.

[EP]

(II)

BAMBOO LANE HOUSE

Sitting alone, hid in bamboo
Plucking the lute and gravely whistling.
People wouldn't know that deep woods
Can be this bright   in the moon.

[GS]

(III)

BAMBOO-MIDST COTTAGE

Sitting alone in recluse bamboo dark
I play a *ch'in*, settle into breath chants.

In these forest depths no one knows
this moon come bathing me in light.

[DH]

DEEP IN THE MOUNTAIN WILDERNESS

Deep in the mountain wilderness
Where nobody ever comes
Only once in a great while
Something like the sound of a far off voice,
The low rays of the sun
Slip through the dark forest,
And gleam again on the shadowy moss.

[KR]

(II)
DEER CAMP

Empty mountains:
    no one to be seen.
Yet—hear—
    human sounds and echoes.
    Returning sunlight
    enters the dark woods;
Again shining
    on green moss, above.

[GS]

(I)
BIRD AND WATERFALL MUSIC

Men sleep. The cassia blossoms fall.
The Spring night is still in the empty mountains.
When the full moon rises,
It troubles the wild birds.
From time to time you can hear them
Above the sound of the flooding waterfalls.

[KR]

(II)
BIRD-CRY CREEK

In our idleness, cinnamon blossoms fall.
In night quiet, spring mountains stand

empty. Moonrise startles mountain birds:
here and there, cries in a spring gorge.

[DH]

In the empty mountains after the new rain
The evening is cool. Soon it will be Autumn.
The bright moon shines between the pines.
The crystal stream flows over the pebbles.
Girls coming home from washing in the river
Rustle through the bamboo grove.
Lotus leaves dance behind the fisherman's boat.
The perfumes of Spring have vanished
But my guests will long remember them.

[KR]

Alighting from my horse to drink with you,
I asked, "Where are you going?"
You said, "Retreating to lie in the southern mountains."
Silent,
I watch the white clouds endless in the distance.

[WCW]

POEM

You who come from my village
Ought to know its affairs
The day you passed the silk window
Had the chill plum bloomed?

[GS]

TWILIGHT COMES

Twilight comes over the monastery garden.
Outside the window the trees grow dim in the dusk.
Woodcutters sing coming home across the fields.
The chant of the monks answers from the forest.
Birds come to the dew basins hidden amongst the flowers.
Off through the bamboos someone is playing a flute.
I am still not an old man,
But my heart is set on the life of a hermit.

[KR]

IN REPLY TO VICE–MAGISTRATE CHANG

In these twilight years, I love tranquillity
alone. Mind free of our ten thousand affairs,

self-regard free of all those grand schemes,
I return to my old forest, knowing empty.

Soon mountain moonlight plays my *ch'in*.
Pine winds loosen my robes. Explain this

inner pattern behind failure and success?
Fishing song carries into shoreline depths.

[DH]

(I)
THE RIVER-MERCHANT'S WIFE: A LETTER

While my hair was still cut straight across my forehead
I played about the front gate, pulling flowers.
You came by on bamboo stilts, playing horse,
You walked about my seat, playing with blue plums.
And we went on living in the village of Chokan:
Two small people, without dislike or suspicion.

At fourteen I married My Lord you.
I never laughed, being bashful.
Lowering my head, I looked at the wall.
Called to, a thousand times, I never looked back.

At fifteen I stopped scowling,
I desired my dust to be mingled with yours
Forever and forever and forever.
Why should I climb the look out?

At sixteen you departed,
You went into far Ku-to-yen, by the river of swirling eddies,
And you have been gone five months.
The monkeys make sorrowful noise overhead.

You dragged your feet when you went out.
By the gate now, the moss is grown, the different mosses,
Too deep to clear them away!
The leaves fall early this autumn, in wind.
The paired butterflies are already yellow with August
Over the grass in the West garden;
They hurt me. I grow older.
If you are coming down through the narrows of the river Kiang,
Please let me know beforehand,
And I will come out to meet you
                    As far as Cho-fu-Sa.

[EP]

II

LONG BANISTER LANE

When my hair was first trimmed across my forehead,
I played in front of my door, picking flowers.
You came riding a bamboo stilt for a horse,
Circling around my yard, playing with green plums.
Living as neighbors at Long Banister Lane,
We had an affection for each other that none were suspicious of.

At fourteen I became your wife,
With lingering shyness, I never laughed.
Lowering my head towards a dark wall,
I never turned, though called a thousand times.

At fifteen I began to show my happiness,
I desired to have my dust mingled with yours.
With a devotion ever unchanging,
Why should I look out when I had you?

At sixteen you left home
For a faraway land of steep pathways and eddies,
Which in May were impossible to traverse,
And where the monkeys whined sorrowfully towards the sky.

The footprints you made when you left the door
Have been covered by green moss,
New moss too deep to be swept away.
The autumn wind came early and the leaves started falling.
The butterflies, yellow with age in August,
Fluttered in pairs towards the western garden.
Looking at the scene, I felt a pang in my heart,
And I sat lamenting my fading youth.

Every day and night I wait for your return,
Expecting to receive your letter in advance,
So that I will come traveling to greet you
As far as Windy Sand.

[WCW]

(III)

CH'ANG-KAN VILLAGE SONG

These bangs not yet reaching my eyes,
I played at our gate, picking flowers,

and you came on your horse of bamboo,
circling the well, tossing green plums.

We lived together here in Ch'ang-kan,
two little people without suspicions.

At fourteen, when I became your wife,
so timid and betrayed I never smiled,

I faced wall and shadow, eyes downcast.
A thousand pleas: I ignored them all.

At fifteen, my scowl began to soften.
I wanted us mingled as dust and ash,

and you always stood fast here for me,
no tower vigils awaiting your return.

At sixteen, you sailed far off to distant
Yen-yü Rock in Ch'ü-t'ang Gorge, fierce

June waters impossible, and howling
gibbons called out into the heavens.

At our gate, where you lingered long,
moss buried your tracks one by one,

deep green moss I can't sweep away.
And autumn's come early. Leaves fall.

It's September now. Butterflies appear
in the west garden. They fly in pairs,

and it hurts. I sit heart-stricken
at the bloom of youth in my old face.

Before you start back from out beyond
all those gorges, send a letter home.

I'm not saying I'd go far to meet you,
no further than Ch'ang-feng Sands.

[DH]

THE JEWEL STAIRS' GRIEVANCE

The jewelled steps are already quite white with dew,
It is so late that the dew soaks my gauze stockings,
And I let down the crystal curtain
And watch the moon through the clear autumn.

[EP]

(II)

JADE-STAIRCASE GRIEVANCE

Night long on the jade staircase, white
dew appears, soaks through gauze stockings.

She lets down crystalline blinds, gazes out
through jewel lacework at the autumn moon.

[DH]

March has come to the bridge head,
Peach boughs and apricot boughs hang over a thousand gates,
At morning there are flowers to cut the heart,
And evening drives them on the eastward-flowing waters.
Petals are on the gone waters and on the going,
        And on the back-swirling eddies,
But to-day's men are not the men of the old days,
Though they hang in the same way over the bridge-rail.
The sea's colour moves at the dawn
And the princes still stand in rows, about the throne,
And the moon falls over the portals of Sei-go-yo,
And clings to the walls and the gate-top.
With head gear glittering against the cloud and sun,
The lords go forth from the court, and into far borders.
They ride upon dragon-like horses,
Upon horses with head-trappings of yellow metal,
And the streets make way for their passage.
        Haughty their passing,
Haughty their steps as they go in to great banquets,
To high halls and curious food,
To the perfumed air and girls dancing,
To clear flutes and clear singing;
To the dance of the seventy couples;
To the mad chase through the gardens.
Night and day are given over to pleasure
And they think it will last a thousand autumns,
        Unwearying autumns.
For them the yellow dogs howl portents in vain,
And what are they compared to the lady Riokushu,
        That was cause of hate!
Who among them is a man like Han-rei
        Who departed alone with his mistress,
With her hair unbound, and he his own skiffsman!

[EP]

LAMENT OF THE FRONTIER GUARD

By the North Gate, the wind blows full of sand,
   Lonely from the beginning of time until now!
   Trees fall, the grass goes yellow with autumn.
   I climb the towers and towers to
             watch out the barbarous land:
Desolate castle, the sky, the wide desert.
There is no wall left to this village.
Bones white with a thousand frosts,
High heaps, covered with trees and grass;
Who bought this to pass?
Who has brought the flaming imperial anger?
Who has brought the army with drums and with kettle-drums?
Barbarous kings.
A gracious spring, tuned to blood-ravenous autumn,
A turmoil of wars-men, spread over the middle kingdom,
Three hundred and sixty thousand.
And sorrow, sorrow like rain.
Sorrow to go, and sorrow, sorrow returning.
Desolate, desolate fields,
And no children of warfare upon them,
     No longer the men for offence and defence.
Ah, how shall you know the dreary sorrow at the North Gate,
With Rihaku's name forgotten,
And we guardsmen fed to the tigers.

                                 [EP]

To So-Kin of Rakuyo, ancient friend, Chancellor of Gen.
Now I remember that you built me a special tavern
By the south side of the bridge at Ten-Shin.
With yellow gold and white jewels, we paid for songs and laughter
And we were drunk for month on month, forgetting the kings and princes.
Intelligent men came drifting in from the sea and from the west border,
And with them, and with you especially
There was nothing at cross purpose,
And they made nothing of sea-crossing or of mountain-crossing,
If only they could be of that fellowship,
And we all spoke out our hearts and minds, and without regret.
And then I was sent off to South Wei,
    smothered in laurel groves,
And you to the north of Raku-hoku,
Till we had nothing but thoughts and memories in common.
And then, when separation had come to its worst,
We met, and travelled into Sen-Go,
Through all the thirty-six folds of the turning and twisting waters,
Into a valley of the thousand bright flowers,
That was the first valley;
And into ten thousand valleys full of voices and pine-winds.
And with silver harness and reins of gold,
Out came the East of Kan foreman and his company.
And there came also the 'True man' of Shi-yo to meet me,
Playing on a jewelled mouth-organ.
In the storied houses of San-Ko they gave us more Sennin music,
Many instruments, like the sound of young phoenix broods.
The foreman of Kan Chu, drunk, danced
    because his long sleeves wouldn't keep still
With that music playing,
And I, wrapped in brocade, went to sleep with my head on his lap,
And my spirit so high it was all over the heavens,
And before the end of the day we were scattered like stars, or rain.
I had to be off to So, far away over the waters,
You back to your river-bridge.

And your father, who was brave as a leopard,
Was governor in Hei-Shu, and put down the barbarian rabble.
And one May he had you send for me,
          despite the long distance.
And what with broken wheels and so on, I won't say it wasn't
          hard going,
Over roads twisted like sheep's guts.
And I was still going, late in the year,
          in the cutting wind from the North,
And thinking how little you cared for the cost,
          and you caring enough to pay it.
And what a reception:
Red jade cups, food well set on a blue jewelled table,
And I was drunk, and had no thought of returning.
And you would walk out with me to the western corner of the castle,
To the dynastic temple, with water about it clear as blue jade,
With boats floating, and the sound of mouth-organs and drums,
With ripples like dragon-scales, going glass green on the water,
Pleasure lasting, with courtezans, going and coming without hindrance,
With the willow flakes falling like snow,
And the vermilioned girls getting drunk about sunset,
And the water, a hundred feet deep, reflecting green eyebrows
—Eyebrows painted green are a fine sight in young moonlight,
Gracefully painted—
And the girls singing back at each other,
Dancing in transparent brocade,
And the wind lifting the song, and interrupting it,
Tossing it up under the clouds.
          And all this comes to an end.
          And is not again to be met with.
I went up to the court for examination,
Tried Layu's luck, offered the Choyo song,
And got no promotion,
          and went back to the East Mountains
          White-headed.
And once again, later, we met at the South bridgehead.
And then the crowd broke up, you went north to San palace,
And if you ask how I regret that parting:

It is like the flowers falling at Spring's end
      Confused, whirled in a tangle.
What is the use of talking, and there is no end of talking,
There is no end of things in the heart.
I call in the boy,
Have him sit on his knees here
      To seal this,
And send it a thousand miles, thinking.

[EP]

TAKING LEAVE OF A FRIEND

Blue mountains to the north of the walls,
White river winding about them;
Here we must make separation
And go out through a thousand miles of dead grass.
Mind like a floating wide cloud,
Sunset like the parting of old acquaintances
Who bow over their clasped hands at a distance.
Our horses neigh to each other
      as we are departing.

[EP]

(I)

SEPARATION ON THE RIVER KIANG

Ko-jin goes west from Ko-kaku-ro,
The smoke-flowers are blurred over the river.
His lone sail blots the far sky.
And now I see only the river,
     The long Kiang, reaching heaven.

[EP]

(II)

ON YELLOW-CRANE TOWER, FAREWELL TO MENG HAO-JAN
WHO'S LEAVING FOR YANG-CHOU

From Yellow-Crane Tower, my old friend leaves the west.
Downstream to Yang-chou, late spring a haze of blossoms,

distant glints of lone sail vanish into emerald-green air:
nothing left but a river flowing on the borders of heaven.

[DH]

WINE

Dew, clear as gilt jewels, hangs under the garden grass-blades.
Swift is the year, swift is the coming cold season,
Life swift as the dart of a bird:

Wine, wine, wine for a hundred autumns,
And then on wine, no wine, and no wine.

[EP]

THE CITY OF CHOAN

The phoenix are at play on their terrace.
The phoenix are gone, the river flows on alone.
Flowers and grass
Cover over the dark path
        where lay the dynastic house of the Go.
The bright cloths and bright caps of Shin
Are now the base of old hills.

The Three Mountains fall through the far heaven,
The isle of White Heron
        splits the two streams apart.
Now the high clouds cover the sun
And I can not see Choan afar
And I am sad.

                                         [EP]

(II)

ON PHOENIX TOWER IN CHIN-LING

In its travels, the phoenix stopped at Phoenix Tower,
but soon left the tower empty, the river flowing away.

Blossoms and grasses burying the paths of a Wu palace,
Chin's capped and robed nobles all ancient gravemounds,

the peaks of Triple Mountain float beyond azure heavens,
and midstream in open waters, White-Egret Island hovers.

It's all drifting clouds and shrouded sun. Lost there,
our Ch'ang-an's nowhere in sight. And so begins grief.

                                         [DH]

SOUTH-FOLK IN COLD COUNTRY

The Dai horse neighs against the bleak wind of Etsu,
The birds of Etsu have no love for En, in the north,
Emotion is born out of habit.
Yesterday we went out of the Wild-Goose gate,
To-day from the Dragon-Pen.
Surprised. Desert turmoil. Sea sun.
Flying snow bewilders the barbarian heaven.
Lice swarm like ants over our accoutrements.
Mind and spirit drive on the feathery banners.
Hard fight gets no reward.
Loyalty is hard to explain.
Who will be sorry for General Rishogu,
      the swift moving,
Whose white head is lost for this province?

                             [EP]

LEAVE-TAKING NEAR SHOKU
'Sanso, King of Shoku, built roads'

They say the roads of Sanso are steep.
Sheer as the mountains.
The walls rise in a man's face,
Clouds grow out of the hill
      at his horse's bridle.
Sweet trees are on the paved way of the Shin,
Their trunks burst through the paving,
And freshets are bursting their ice
      in the midst of Shoku, a proud city.

Men's fates are already set,
There is no need of asking diviners.

                             [EP]

The red sun comes out of the Eastern corner
  as if he sprang from the bottom of the earth
It crosses heaven and sinks again in the sea
Who will say where the six dragons of his car will come to rest
Who will date its beginning and ending
Man, who art not a cardinal spirit
How shall you think to wander forever with the
  unwearying sun, yourself unwearied
How shall you desire it
Yet the grass takes no thought of the wind that makes it flourish
The trees do not hate the autumn of their decline
Who by brandishing whips will hasten the course of the seasons?
Or of the myriad things that
  without thought arise and decay

                                      [EP]

SONG FOR THE FALLING KINGDOM

Homing crows drift in the air at nest time
        over the terrace at Koso,
Within, the Go king is drinking with Sei-shi,
The song of his dynasty has not yet run to its end
        Nor her dances danced to a finish
        The Blue Mountain bathes in the sun
        Pale rays still strike the gold urn
        and fall slowly into the water.
The autumn moonlight is already tinging the river,
        What use is this pleasure tomorrow.

                                        [EP]

SPRING SONG

A young lass
Plucks mulberry leaves by the river

Her white hand
Reaches among the green

Her flushed cheeks
Shine under the sun

The hungry silkworms
Are waiting

Oh, young horseman
Why do you tarry. Get going.

[WCW]

SUMMER SONG

The Mirror Lake
　　(Three hundred miles),

Where lotus buds
　　Burst into flowers.

The slippery shore
　　Is jammed with admirers,

While the village beauty
　　Picks the blossoms.

Before the sails
　　Breast the rising moon,

She's shipped away
　　To the king's harem.

[WCW]

(I)
DRINKING TOGETHER

We drink in the mountain while the flowers bloom,
A pitcher, a pitcher, and one more pitcher.
As my head spins you get up.
So be back any time with your guitar.

[WCW]

(II)
DRINKING IN THE MOUNTAINS WITH A RECLUSE

Drinking together among mountain blossoms, we
down a cup, another, and yet another. Soon drunk,

I fall asleep, and you wander off. Tomorrow morning,
if you think of it, grab your *ch'in* and come again.

[DH]

WANDERING CH'ING-LING STREAM IN NAN-YANG

I hoard the sky a setting sun leaves
and love this cold stream's clarity:

western light follows water away,
rippled current a wanderer's heart.

I sing, watch cloud and moon, empty
song soon long wind through pine.

[DH]

WAR SOUTH OF THE GREAT WALL

War last year at Sang-kan's headwaters,
war this year on the roads at Ts'ung River:

we've rinsed weapons clean in T'iao-chih sea-swells,
pastured horses in T'ien Mountain's snowbound grasses,

war in ten-thousand-mile campaigns
leaving our Three Armies old and broken,

but the Hsiung-nu have made slaughter their own version of plowing.
It never changes: nothing since ancient times but bleached bones in
     fields of yellow sand.

A Ch'in emperor built the Great Wall to seal Mongols out,
and still, in the Han, we're setting beacon fires ablaze.

Beacon fires ablaze everlasting,
no end to forced marches and war,

it's fight to the death in outland war,
wounded horses wailing, crying out toward heaven,

hawks and crows tearing at people,
lifting off to scatter dangling entrails in dying trees.

Tangled grasses lie matted with death,
but generals keep at it. And for what?

Isn't it clear that weapons are the tools of misery?
The great sages never waited until the need for such things arose.

[DH]

(I)

A LETTER

My love,
        When you were here there was
            a hall of flowers.
When you are gone there is
    an empty bed.
Under the embroidered coverlet
    I toss and turn.
After three years I
    smell your fragrance.
Your fragrance never leaves,
But you never return.
I think of you, the yellow leaves are ended
And the white dew dampens the green moss.

[WCW]

(II)

TO SEND FAR AWAY

So much beauty home—flowers filled the house.
So much beauty gone—nothing but this empty bed,

your embroidered quilt rolled up, never used.
It's been three years. Your scent still lingers,

your scent gone and yet never ending.
But now you're gone, never to return,

thoughts of you yellow leaves falling,
white dew glistening on green moss.

[DH]

THINKING OF EAST MOUNTAIN

It's forever since I faced East Mountain.
How many times have roses bloomed there,

or clouds returned, and thinned away,
a bright moon setting over whose home?

[DH]

ON HSIN-P'ING TOWER

On this tower as I leave our homeland,
late autumn wounds thoughts of return,

and heaven long, a setting sun far off,
this cold clear river keeps flowing away.

Chinese clouds rise from mountain forests;
Mongol geese on sandbars take flight.

A million miles azure pure—the eye
reaches beyond what ruins our lives.

[DH]

MOUNTAIN DIALOGUE

You ask why I've settled in these emerald mountains:
I smile, mind of itself perfectly idle, and say nothing.

Peach blossoms drift streamwater away deep in mystery
here, another heaven and earth, nowhere people know.

[DH]

WRITTEN ON A WALL AT HSIU-CHING
MONASTERY IN WU-CH'ANG

Now a monastery on southern river-banks,
this was once my northen kinsman's home.

There's no one like him now. Courtyards
empty, monks sit deep in temple silence.

His books remain, bound in ribbon-grass,
and white dust blankets his *ch'in* stand.

He lived simply, planting peach and plum,
but in nirvana, springtime never arrives.

[DH]

(I)

THOUGHTS IN NIGHT QUIET

Seeing moonlight here at my bed,
and thinking it's frost on the ground,

I look up, gaze at the mountain moon,
then back, dreaming of my old home.

[DH]

(II)

CALM NIGHT THOUGHT

The moon light is on the floor luminous
I thought it was frost, it was so white
Holding up head I look at mountain moon
that makes me lower head
lowering head think of old home

alternate lines:

mountain
looking up I find it to be the moon

[EP]

A MOUNTAIN SPRING

There is a brook in the mountains,
Nobody I ask knows its name.
It shines on the earth like a piece
Of the sky. It falls away
In waterfalls, with a sound
Like rain. It twists between rocks
And makes deep pools. It divides
Into islands. It flows through
Calm reaches. It goes its way
With no one to mind it. The years
Go by, its clear depths never change.

[KR]

TEA

By noon the heat became unbearable.
The birds stopped flying
And went to roost exhausted.
Sit here in the shade of the big tree.
Take off your hot woolen jacket.
The few small clouds floating overhead
Do nothing to cool the heat of the sun.
I'll put some tea on to boil
And cook some vegetables.
It's a good thing you don't live far.
You can stroll home after sunset.

[KR]

CHANT OF THE FRONTIERSMAN

I

The cicadas are singing in the mulberry forest:
It is August at the fortress.
We pass the frontiers to enter more frontiers.
Everywhere the rushes are yellow.

The sodbusters from the provinces
Have disappeared with the dust they kicked up.
Why should we bother to be knights-errant?
Let us discuss the merits of bayards.

II

I lead the horse to drink in the autumn river.
The river is icy and the wind cuts like knives.
In the desert the sun has not yet gone down;
In the shade I see my distant home.

When the war first spread to the Great Wall,
We were filled with patriotic fervor.
The yellow sand has covered the past glories;
The bleached bones are scattered over the nettles.

[WCW]

PARTING WITH HSIN CHIEN AT HIBISCUS TAVERN

Cold rain on the river
    we enter Wu by night
At dawn I leave
    for Ch'u-shan, alone.
If friends in Lo-yang
    ask after me, I've
"A heart like ice
    in a jade vase."

[GS]

(I)

WRITTEN ON THE WALL AT CHANG'S HERMITAGE

It is Spring in the mountains.
I come alone seeking you.
The sound of chopping wood echoes
Between the silent peaks.
The streams are still icy.
There is snow on the trail.
At sunset I reach your grove
In the stony mountain pass.
You want nothing, although at night
You can see the aura of gold
And silver ore all around you.
You have learned to be gentle
As the mountain deer you have tamed.
The way back forgotten, hidden
Away, I become like you,
An empty boat, floating, adrift.

[KR]

(II)

WRITTEN ON THE WALL AT CHANG'S RECLUSE HOME

In spring mountains, alone, I set out to find you.
Axe strokes crack—crack and quit. Silence doubles.

I pass snow and ice lingering along cold streams,
then, at Stone-Gate in late light, enter these woods.

You harm nothing: deer roam here each morning;
want nothing: auras gold and silver grace nights.

Facing you on a whim in bottomless dark, the way
here lost—I feel it drifting, this whole empty boat.

[DH]

War-carts clatter and creak,
horses stomp and splutter—
each wearing quiver and bow, the war-bound men pass.
Mothers and fathers, wives and children—they all flock
alongside, farewell dust so thick Hsien-yang Bridge
disappears. They get everywhere in the way, crying

cries to break against heaven, tugging at war clothes.
On the roadside, when a passerby asks war-bound men,
war-bound men say simply: *Our lots are drawn often.*
Taken north at fifteen, we guard the Yellow River. Taken
west at forty, we man frontier camps. Village elders
tied our head-cloths then. And now we return, our
hair white, only to be sent out again to borderlands,

lands where blood swells like sea-water. And Emperor Wu's
imperial dreams of conquest roll on. Haven't you heard
that east of the mountains, in our Han
                            homeland, ten hundred towns and
ten thousand villages are overrun by thorned weeds,
that even though strong wives keep hoeing and plowing,
you can't tell where crops are and aren't? It's worst for
mighty Ch'in warriors: the more bitter war they outlive,
the more they are herded about like chickens and dogs.
Though you are kind to ask, sir,
how could we complain? Imagine
this winter in Ch'in. Their men
still haven't returned, and those
clerks are out demanding taxes.

Taxes! How could they pay taxes?
Even a son's birth is tragic now.
People prefer a daughter's birth,
a daughter's birth might at least end in marriage nearby.
But a son's birth ends in an open grave who knows

where. You haven't seen how bones from ancient times
lie, bleached and unclaimed along the shores of
Sky-Blue Seas—how the weeping of old ghosts is
joined by new voices, the gray sky by twittering rain.

[DH]

(I)

SNOW STORM

Tumult, weeping, many new ghosts.
Heartbroken, aging, alone, I sing
To myself. Ragged mist settles
In the spreading dusk. Snow skurries
In the coiling wind. The wineglass
Is spilled. The bottle is empty.
The fire has gone out in the stove.
Everywhere men speak in whispers.
I brood on the uselessness of letters.

[KR]

(II)

FACING SNOW

Enough new ghosts now to mourn any war,
And a lone old grief-sung man. Clouds at
Twilight's ragged edge foundering, wind
Buffets a dance of headlong snow. A ladle

Lies beside this jar drained of emerald
Wine. The stove's flame-red mirage lingers.
News comes from nowhere. I sit here,
Spirit-wounded, tracing words onto air.

[DH]

P'ENG-YA SONG

I remember long ago slipping away
in precarious depths of night. The moon
bright on Po-shui Mountain, I eluded
rebel armies and fled with my family

far north by foot on P'eng-ya Road.
By then, most people we met had lost all
shame. Scattered bird cries haunted
valleys. No one returned the way we came.

My silly, starved girl bit me and screamed.
Afraid tigers and wolves might hear,
I cradled her close, holding her mouth,
but she squirmed loose, crying louder still.

Looking after us gallantly, my little boy
searched out sour-plum feasts. Of ten days,
half were all thunder and rain—mud
and more mud to drag ourselves through.

We didn't plan for rain. Clothes ever
colder, the road slippery, an insufferable
day's travel often took us but a few short
miles by nightfall. Wild fruit replaced

what little food we had carried with us.
Low branches became our home. We left dew-
splashed rocks each morning, and passed
night at the smoke-scored edge of heaven.

We had stopped at T'ung-chia Marsh,
planning to cross Lu-tzu Pass, when you
took us in, Sun Tsai, old friend, your
kindness towering like billowing clouds.

Dusk already become night, you hung lanterns
out and swung door after door wide open.
You soothed our feet with warm water
and cut paper charms to summon our souls,

then called your wife and children in, their
eyes filling with tears for us. My chicks
soon drifted away in sleep, but you brought
them back, offering choice dishes of food.

You and I, you promised, will be forever
bound together like two dear brothers.
And before long, you emptied our rooms,
leaving us to joy and peace and rest.

In these times overrun with such calamity,
how many hearts are so open and generous?
A year of months since we parted, and still
those Mongols spin their grand catastrophes.

How long before I've grown feathers and wings
and settled beside you at the end of flight?

[DH]

SPRING VIEW

The nation is ruined,   but mountains and rivers remain.
This spring the city   is deep in weeds and brush.
Touched by the times   even flowers weep tears,
Fearing leaving   the birds tangled hearts.
Watch-tower fires   have been burning for three months
To get a note from home   would cost ten thousand gold.
Scratching my   white hair thinner
Seething hopes   all in a trembling hairpin.

[GS]

TO LI PO

The floating cloud follows the sun.
The traveler has not yet returned.
For three nights I dreamt of you, my friend,
So clearly that I almost touched you.

You left me in a hurry.
Your passage is fraught with trouble:
The wind blows fiercely over lakes and rivers.
Be watchful lest you fall from your boat!
You scratched your white head when leaving the door,
And I knew the journey was against your wishes.

Silk-hatted gentlemen have swamped the capital,
While you, the poet, are lean and haggard.
If the net of heaven is not narrow,
Why should you be banished when you are old?
Ten thousand ages will remember your warmth;
When you are gone the world is silent and cold.

[WCW]

DREAMING OF LI PO

Death at least gives separation repose.
Without death, its grief can only sharpen.
You wander out in malarial southlands,
and I hear nothing of you, exiled

old friend. Knowing I think of you
always now, you visit my dreams, my heart
frightened it is no living spirit
I dream. Endless miles—you come

so far from the Yangtze's sunlit maples
night shrouds the passes when you return.
And snared as you are in their net,
with what bird's wings could you fly?

Filling my room to the roof-beams, the moon
sinks. You nearly linger in its light,
but the waters deepen in long swells,
unfed dragons—take good care old friend.

[DH]

VISIT

In life we could seldom meet
Separate as the stars.
What a special occasion tonight
That we gather under the candle-lamp!

How long can youth last?
Our hair is peppered with white.
Half of our friends are ghosts
It's so good to see you alive.

How strange after twenty years
To revisit your house!
When I left you were single
Your children are grown up now.
They treat me with great respect,
Ask where I came from.

Before I can answer
You send your son for the wine.
In the rain you cut scallions
And start the oven to cook rice.

"It's so hard to get together
Let's finish up these ten goblets."
After ten goblets we are still sober
The feeling of reunion is long.

Tomorrow I have to cross the mountain
Back to the mist of the world.

[WCW]

TO WEI PA, A RETIRED SCHOLAR

The lives of many men are
Shorter than the years since we have
Seen each other. Aldebaran
And Antares move as we have.
And now, what night is this? We sit
Here together in the candle
Light. How much longer will our prime
Last? Our temples are already
Grey. I visit my old friends.
Half of them have become ghosts.
Fear and sorrow choke me and burn
My bowels. I never dreamed I would
Come this way, after twenty years,
A wayfarer to your parlor.
When we parted years ago,
You were unmarried. Now you have
A row of boys and girls, who smile
And ask me about my travels.
How have I reached this time and place?
Before I can come to the end
Of an endless tale, the children
Have brought out the wine. We go
Out in the night and cut young
Onions in the rainy darkness.
We eat them with hot, steaming,
Yellow millet. You say, "It is
Sad, meeting each other again."

We drink ten toasts rapidly from
The rhinoceros horn cups.
Ten cups, and still we are not drunk.
We still love each other as
We did when we were schoolboys.
Tomorrow morning mountain peaks
Will come between us, and with them
The endless, oblivious
Business of the world.

[KR]

FOR THE RECLUSE WEI PA

Lives two people live drift without
meeting, like Scorpio and Orion,
without nights like this: two friends
together again, candles and lamps

flickering. And youth doesn't last.
Already gray, we ask after old friends,
finding ghosts—everywhere, ghosts.
It startles the heart, and twists there.

Who dreamed it would be twenty years
when I left? You weren't married then,
and look—already a proper little
flock of sons and daughters. In gleeful

respect for their father's friend, they
ask where I've come from. And before
the asking and telling end, they are
bundled off to help with soup and wine,

spring scallions cut fresh in evening rain,
steamed rice garnished with yellow millet.
Pronouncing reunions extinct, you pour
ten cups a throw *to our health*. Ten cups,

and I'm drunk on nothing like your unfailing
friendship. Tomorrow, between us in all
this clamor of consequence, mountain
peaks will open out across two distances.

[DH]

MOON FESTIVAL

The Autumn constellations
Begin to rise. The brilliant
Moonlight shines on the crowds.
The moon toad swims in the river
And does not drown. The moon rabbit
Pounds the bitter herbs of the
Elixir of eternal life.
His drug only makes my heart
More bitter. The silver brilliance
Only makes my hair more white.
I know that the country is
Overrun with war. The moonlight
Means nothing to the soldiers
Camped in the western deserts.

[KR]

MOONLIT NIGHT THINKING OF MY BROTHERS

Warning drums have ended all travel.
A lone goose cries across autumn
Borderlands. White Dew begins tonight,
This bright moon bright there, over

My old village. My scattered brothers—
And no home to ask *Are they alive or dead?*
Letters never arrive. War comes
And goes—then comes like this again.

[DH]

TRAVELING NORTHWARD

Screech owls moan in the yellowing
Mulberry trees. Field mice scurry,
Preparing their holes for winter.
Midnight, we cross an old battlefield.
The moonlight shines cold on white bones.

[KR]

STANDING ALONE

Empty skies. And beyond, one hawk.
Between river banks, two white gulls
Drift and flutter. Fit for an easy kill,
To and fro, they follow contentment.

Dew shrouds grasses. Spiderwebs are still
Not gathered in. The purpose driving
Heaven become human now, I stand where
Uncounted sorrows begin beginning alone.

[DH]

LANDSCAPE

Clear autumn opens endlessly away.
Early shadows deepening, distant
Waters empty into flawless sky.
A lone city lies lost in fog. Few

Enough leaves, and wind scattering
More, the sun sets over remote peaks.
A lone crane returning. . . . Why so late?
Crows already glut woods with night.

[DH]

TO PI SSU YAO

We have talent. People call us
The leading poets of our day.
Too bad, our homes are humble,
Our recognition trivial.
Hungry, ill clothed, servants treat
Us with contempt. In the prime
Of life, our faces are wrinkled.
Who cares about either of us,
Or our troubles? We are our own
Audience. We appreciate
Each other's literary
Merits. Our poems will be handed
Down along with great dead poets'.
We can console each other.
At least we shall have descendants.

[KR]

OUTSIDE THE CITY

It is bitter cold, and late, and falling
Dew muffles my gaze into bottomless skies.
Smoke trails out over distant salt mines
Where snow-covered peaks cast shadows east.

Armies haunt my homeland still. And war
Drums throb in this distant place. A guest
Overnight in a river city, together with
Shrieking crows, my old friends, I return.

[DH]

(I)

I PASS THE NIGHT AT GENERAL HEADQUARTERS

A clear night in harvest time.
In the courtyard at headquarters
The wu-tung trees grow cold.
In the city by the river
I wake alone by a guttering
Candle. All night long bugle
Calls disturb my thoughts. The splendor
Of the moonlight floods the sky.
Who bothers to look at it?
Whirlwinds of dust, I cannot write.
The frontier pass is unguarded.
It is dangerous to travel.
Ten years wandering, sick at heart.
I perch here like a bird on a
Twig, thankful for a moment's peace.

[KR]

(II)

OVERNIGHT AT HEADQUARTERS

Clear autumn. Beside the well, cold *wu* trees. I pass
Night in the river city, alone, candles guttering low.

Grieving in the endless dark, horns call to themselves.
The moon drifts—no one to see its exquisite color.

Wind and dust, one calamity after another. And frontier
Passes all desolation and impossible roads, no news

Arrives. After ten desperate, headlong years, driven
Perch to perch, I cling to what peace one twig holds.

[DH]

(I)
A RESTLESS NIGHT IN CAMP

In the penetrating damp
I sleep under the bamboos,
Under the penetrating
Moonlight in the wilderness.
The thick dew turns to fine mist.
One by one the stars go out.
Only the fireflies are left.
Birds cry over the water.
War breeds its consequences.
It is useless to worry,
Wakeful while the long night goes.

[KR]

(II)
RESTLESS NIGHT

As bamboo chill drifts into the bedroom,
Moonlight fills every corner of our
Garden. Heavy dew beads and trickles.
Stars suddenly there, sparse, next aren't.

Fireflies in dark flight flash. Waking
Waterbirds begin calling, one to another.
All things caught between shield and sword,
All grief empty, the clear night passes.

[DH]

(I)
BRIMMING WATER

Under my feet the moon
Glides along the river.
Near midnight, a gusty lantern
Shines in the heart of night.
Along the sandbars flocks
Of white egrets roost,
Each one clenched like a fist.
In the wake of my barge
The fish leap, cut the water,
And dive and splash.

[KR]

(II)
BRIMMED WHOLE

A river moon only feet away, storm-lanterns
alight late in the second watch . . . . Serene

flock of fists on sand—egrets asleep when
a fish leaps in the boat's wake, shivering, cry.

[DH]

FULL MOON

Above the tower—a lone, twice-sized moon.
On the cold river passing night-filled homes,
It scatters restless gold across waves.
On mats, it shines richer than silken gauze.

Empty peaks, silence: among sparse stars,
Not yet flawed, it drifts. Pine and cinnamon
Spreading in my old garden. . . . All light,
All ten thousand miles at once in its light!

[DH]

THATCH HOUSE

Our thatch house perched where land ends,
we leave the brushwood gate always open.

Dragons and fish settle into evening waters.
Moon and stars drifting above autumn peaks,

dew gathers clarity, then thaws. High clouds
thin away—none return. Women man wind-

tossed boats anchored here: young, ashamed,
that river life battering their warm beauty.

[DH]

DAWN OVER THE MOUNTAINS

The city is silent,
Sound drains away,
Buildings vanish in the light of dawn,
Cold sunlight comes on the highest peak,
The thick dust of night
Clings to the hills,
The earth opens,
The river boats are vague,
The still sky—
The sound of falling leaves.
A huge doe comes to the garden gate,
Lost from the herd,
Seeking its fellows.

[KR]

(II)

DAWN LANDSCAPE

The last watch has sounded in K'uei-chou.
Color spreading above Sun-Terrace Mountain,

a cold sun clears high peaks. Clouds linger,
blotting out canyons below tangled ridges,

and deep Yangtze banks keep sails hidden.
Beneath clear skies: clatter of falling leaves.

And these deer at my bramble gate: so close
here, we touch our own kind in each other.

[DH]

from THOUGHTS

1
Throughout Heaven and Earth, whatever lives
contends. Each place has its own way,
but we all struggle inchmeal, one with another,
tangling ourselves ever tighter in the snare.

Without aristocracy, what would the lowly
grieve for? And without wealth, what could
poverty lack? O, neighborhoods may take turns
mourning, but all time is one lone corpse.

Here, in Wu Gorge, I have lived three unkempt
years out like a fluttering candle, blessed that
after a lifetime growing content with failure,
I've forgotten how splendor and disgrace differ.

Chosen for court or grown old in some outland,
I need the same workaday rice. But here, my
house of woven bramble east of city walls, I can
pick healing herbs in shaded mountain valleys.

Searching out roots beneath frost and snow,
I wear my heart away without thinking of lush
branches and vines. It isn't discipline—
this quiet life apart has always been my joy.

They say a sage is taut as a bowstring and
a fool is bent hookwise. Who knows which
I am? Taut hookwise, warming my old back
here in the sun, I await woodcutters and herdsmen.

[DH]

NIGHT THOUGHTS WHILE TRAVELING

A light breeze rustles the reeds
Along the river banks. The
Mast of my lonely boat soars
Into the night. Stars blossom
Over the vast desert of
Waters. Moonlight flows on the
Surging river. My poems have
Made me famous but I grow
Old, ill and tired, blown hither
And yon; I am like a gull
Lost between heaven and earth.

[KR]

THOUGHTS, TRAVELING AT NIGHT

In delicate beach-grass, a slight breeze.
The boat's mast teetering up into solitary
Night, plains open away beneath foundering stars.
A moon emerges and, the river vast, flows.

How will poems bring honor? My career
Lost to age and sickness, buffeted, adrift
On the wind—is there anything like it? All
Heaven and earth, and one lone sand-gull.

[DH]

CH'IEN CH'I

VISIT TO THE HERMIT TS'UI

Moss covered paths between scarlet peonies,
Pale jade mountains fill your rustic windows.
I envy you, drunk with flowers,
Butterflies swirling in your dreams.

[KR]

(I)

NIGHT AT ANCHOR BY MAPLE BRIDGE

The moon sets. A crow caws.
Frost fills the sky.
Maple leaves fall on the river.
The fishermen's fires keep me awake.
From beyond Su Chou
The midnight bell on Cold Mountain
Reaches as far as my little boat.

[KR]

(II)

MAPLE BRIDGE NIGHT MOORING

Moon set, a crow caws,
        frost fills the sky
River, maple, fishing-fires
        cross my troubled sleep.
Beyond the walls of Su-chou
        from Cold Mountain temple
The midnight bell sounds
        reach my boat.

[GS]

CHAO LUAN-LUAN

SLENDER FINGERS

Slender, delicate, soft jade,
Fresh peeled spring onions—
They are always hidden in emerald
Sleeves of perfumed silk.
Yesterday on the lute strings
All their nails were painted scarlet.

[KR]

RED SANDALWOOD MOUTH

Small cherries sip delicately
At the edge of the wine cup.
Beautiful speech floats on jasmine perfume.
Like the mouth of the singer Fan Su,
The concubine of Po Chü-i,
The teeth are like white melon seeds,
And the lips like pomegranate blossoms.

[KR]

WILLOW EYEBROWS

Sorrows play at the edge of these willow leaf curves.
They are often reflected, deep, deep,
In my water blossom inlaid mirror.
I am too pretty to bother with an eyebrow pencil.
Spring hills paint themselves
With their own personality.

[KR]

CREAMY BREASTS

Fragrant with powder, moist with perspiration,
They are the pegs of a jade inlaid harp.
Aroused by spring, they are soft as cream
Under the fertilizing mist.
After my bath my perfumed lover
Holds them and plays with them
And they are cool as peonies and purple grapes.

[KR]

from MOURNING LU YIN

1

Invariably pure and austere, poets mostly
starve to death embracing empty mountains,

and when white clouds have no master,
they just drift off, idle thoughts carefree.

Servants too weak to make arrangements
after a long illness, your body lies waiting

among all those prize books hungry mice
shredded and scattered through the house.

You've gone to the village of new ghosts
now. I look into a face white as old jade,

then watch your burial, ashamed no one
follows, clutching at you, calling you back.

At dusk, springs mourn by the hundred,
their empty lament flowing and flowing.

2

Hush of a loom's shuttle over and over,
one moon lights a thousand forevers

gone. All purity fresh again and again,
one spring blossoms a thousand forevers

gone, forever gone. Graveyard winds
my lament, Sung Mountain autumn's

now your tomb. And everywhere here,
all dust and dirt, graveyard guests

mourn, thorns and brambles voicing
bitter grief born of tear-soaked roots.

Where even fire couldn't warm itself,
the body's force fails quickly. Silent,

alone, I offer a cup of tears, start it
toward the clear Lo River, adding this

heart-stricken cry to that never-ending
sound of death dragging people apart.

3
Thorn-bramble winds keep calling out,
splintering all that bitter lament apart,

bitter lament no one could bear. You
cover your ears, but it keeps coming,

chords of sorrow, so many searing cries
over such lavish loss. The spirit's charred

mourning poverty, and mourning death
fires the heart to sheer ash. A moment's

shimmering dream, the world drifts deep
eddies of swelling tears. Burial songs

sung once, you're gone. And once weeds
close you in, they'll never open again.

[DH]

1

Long ago, everyone laughed together,
but who's left to share this lament now,

lament of the gorges shadowy spirits
mourning. Winds howl. Sinking ghosts

embrace an empty moon, disappearing,
appearing—they can't stop themselves.

Pounding us to dust in a lightning flash,
spring's thundering thousand-foot swells

flood these gorges with sound, dragging
jade-pure currents through whirlpool

clarities. Riverbanks battered and awash,
sawtooth waves open. Snarling, snarling

and gaping bottomless, a swilling lure,
they promise unfathomed catastrophe,

spewing out the valley's brimful cries,
swirling embattled around rock's fury.

Long ago, they sent felons back home.
Now this prison's taking so many of us,

orphaned words empty resemblances,
each mouthful of snow startling still.

People shabby and low, true hearts few,
it's money makes friends. Yellow gold

buys you mourners. They've soon gone
home, though, their tears already dry.

But I mind the heart's old ways: for you,
emptiness broken and scattered away.

2
Water all heaven-above heaven-below,
a boat leaves earth entering earth here.

Swordblades of rock slice at each other,
rock-broken waves all angry dragons,

and though blossoms rekindle spring,
freezing winds make autumn timeless.

Unearthly voices rise from hidden dens.
Flies thicken, buzzing currents in flight.

The sun sunk deep, drowning lament,
how could we set out pleading for help?

3
Triple Gorge one thread of heaven over
ten thousand cascading thongs of water,

slivers of sun and moon sheering away
above, and wild swells walled-in below,

splintered spirits glisten, a few glints
frozen how many hundred years in dark

gorges midday light never finds, gorges
hungry froth fills with peril. Rotting

coffins locked into tree roots, isolate
bones twist and sway, dangling free,

and grieving frost roosts in branches,
keeping lament's dark, distant harmony

fresh. Exile, tattered heart all scattered
away, you'll simmer in seething flame

here, your life like fine-spun thread,
its road a trace of string traveled away.

Offer tears to mourn the water-ghosts,
and water-ghosts take them, glimmering.

4
Young clear-voiced dragons in these
gorges howl. Fresh scales born of rock,

they spew froth of fetid rain, breath
heaving, churning up black sinkholes.

Strange new lights glint, and hungry
swords await. This venerable old maw

still hasn't eaten its fill. Ageless teeth
cry a fury of cliffs, cascades gnawing

through these three gorges, gorges
full of jostling and snarling, snarling.

5
In gorges, dragons voice age-old explanations.
In pools ten hundred feet deep, you hear them.

Cruel waves keep strict accounts, drinking
blood to nurture children and grandchildren,

but without ancient Kao Yao's gentle justice,
feasting on prison-drowned spirits is empty.

Something there, mystery haunting darkness,
the futile talk of ghosts goes on and ever on,

gorges hearing cascades cry lament, gorges
mourning widowed gibbons. There's nothing

human in the sound of gorges, gorges where
blades of churning water slice at themselves,

and now, sage hearts all hidden away here,
who marshals these bitter and drowned pleas?

6
These gorges a dragon's heart of lies,
loudmouth banks thirsty for accusation,

there's nothing honest in this feeding,
this voice brimful of such rank noise.

Rock teeth chewing a hundred streams,
rock winds singing a thousand *ch'in*,

you can't stay free of its isolate lament,
can't sort through this crack in snow.

Majestic spirit drifts high in the moon,
but deep in the clarity of gorges, dragon

dens endure. You can't embrace its pain,
and our pleas never shine clear. Empty

swordblades, flying billows and swells
carve a thousand peaks from solid rock.

7
Upper edges of these gorges shattering
sun and moon, sun and moon altogether

splintered light, things grow all tilted
away here, and birds tilt away in flight.

Hidden rocks locking teeth, summoned
spirits never return from these depths.

Wild flurries of armor, clear streams
clothe jade-pure rock in shimmering

color. And hungrily swallowed cascades
thunder, frothing like swirling grease.

You can't wander spring gorges: fetid
grasses already spread such lean stains.

8
Light flowing in gorges plays across cliffs,
shapes changing, blossoms spectral without

spring. Hidden among roots, jade-pure rain
gracing river crossings, froth blazes red.

This canyon dragon-hearted, river demons
people villages. Feeding on whatever lives,

they don't care if you're noble and wise.
We all nurse our lives into death alone,

nothing to trust among all our fetid words,
songs forced, happiness a sham. Unearthly

crops missing, fields tilt away, and savage
scales fill these poison waters. You can't

make such unearthly things friends, can't
work out lament in laments of the gorges.

9
Water swords and spears raging in gorges,
boats drift across heaving thunder. Here

in the hands of these serpents and snakes,
you face everyday frenzies of wind and rain,

and how many fleeing exiles travel these
gorges, gorges rank inhabitants people?

You won't find a heart beneath this sheen,
this flood that's stored away aftermath

forever. Arid froth raising boundless mist,
froth all ablaze and snarling, snarling—

what of that thirst for wisdom when you're
suddenly here, dead center in these waters?

10
Death-owls call in human voices. Dragons
wolf down heaving mountain waters. Here

in broad daylight, with all the enticing
serenity of a clear and breezy sky, they

beggar wisdom, snarling everything alive
in fetid gatherings of vine-covered depths.

Want filling fanged cascades bottomless,
sawtooth froth swells everywhere. Nesting

birds can't settle in trees tilted so askew,
trees gibbons leaping and swinging fill.

Who can welcome laments of the gorges,
gorges saying *What will come will come.*

[DH]

Yin-yo laps in the reeds, my guest departs,
The maple leaves blot up their shadows,
The sky is full of autumn,
We drink our parting in saki.
Out of the night comes troubling lute music,
And we cry out, asking the singer's name,
And get this answer:
                    "Many a one
Brought me rich presents; my hair was full of jade,
And my slashed skirts, drenched in expensive dyes,
Were dipped in crimson, sprinkled with rare wines.
I was well taught my arts at Ga-ma-rio,
And then one year I faded out and married."
The lute-bowl hid her face.
                    We heard her weeping.

[EP]

THE BAMBOO BY LI CH'E YUN'S WINDOW

Don't cut it to make a flute.
Don't trim it for a fishing
Pole. When the grass and flowers
Are all gone, it will be beautiful
Under the falling snow flakes.

[KR]

PALACE SONG

Tears soak her thin shawl
    dreams won't come.
In the dark night, from the front palace,
    girls rehearsing songs.
Still fresh and young,
    already put down,
She leans across the brazier
    to wait the coming dawn.

                                [GS]

VILLAGE SNOW, SITTING AT NIGHT

At the south window, my back to a lamp,
I sit. Wind scatters sleet into darkness.

In lone depths of silent village night:
the call of a late goose in falling snow.

                                [DH]

AT FLOWERING-BRIGHTNESS MONASTERY
IN YUNG-CH'UNG DISTRICT

It's late summer weather, time bitter
heat begins to ease: windblown trees

murmur under skies promising rain,
and at dusk, cicadas cry on and on.

Narrow Yung-ch'ung streets quiet,
temple gardens all isolate mystery,

no one visits. Autumn scholartree
blossoms blanket the ground. Here,

the lit years pass, careless and slow,
the world's great dramas far away.

Why wait until I'm feeble to realize
our life's elusive, our death repose?

A true recluse need not live far away
knowing Tao is groping in darkness:

even in the world's bustle and dust
a mind of emptiness never wanders.

Fresh vegetables for dawn hunger
and fur-lined robes for chill nights:

such luck to elude hunger and cold.
What more could I ever ask? Simple

and hardly sick—this is all I want.
Rejoice in heaven, resent nothing:

how could I explain such resolve?
An *I Ching*'s lying beside the bed.

[DH]

AUTUMN THOUGHTS, SENT FAR AWAY

We share all these disappointments of failing
autumn a thousand miles apart. This is where

autumn wind easily plunders courtyard trees,
but the sorrows of distance never scatter away.

Swallow shadows shake out homeward wings.
Orchid scents thin, drifting from old thickets.

These lovely seasons and fragrant years falling
lonely away—we share such emptiness here.

[DH]

NIGHT IN THE PALACE WITH CH'IEN HUI

When the water-clock sounds three times, I realize it's midnight.
Lovely wind and cold moonlight everywhere in pine and bamboo,

we sit here in perfect idleness, empty and still, saying nothing:
just two people in the shadows of a medicine tree, just two people.

[DH]

WINTER NIGHT

Those I love scattered away, poor
and far too sick for friendly visits,

I'm shut up inside, no one in sight.
Lying in this village study alone,

the wick cold and lampflame dark,
wide open drapes torn and tattered,

I listen as the snow begins to fall
again, that hiss outside the window.

Older now, sleeping less and less,
I get up in the night and sit intent,

mind utterly forgotten. How else
can I get past such isolate silence?

Body visiting this world steadfast,
mind abandoned to change limitless:

it's been like this four years now,
one thousand three hundred nights.

[DH]

DREAMING OF LONG AGO

I've grown old since our farewell, bitterly cultivating the Tao,
refining this irreconcilable heart all the way into dead ash.

I thought I'd polished the memories of a lifetime clean away—
so how is it you came stealing into my dreams again last night?

[DH]

VISITING THE RECLUSE CHENG

Having fathomed Tao, you went to dwell among simple villages
where bamboo grows thick, opening and closing your gate alone.

This isn't a mission or pilgrimage. I've come for no real reason:
just to sit out on your south terrace and gaze at those mountains.

[DH]

IDLE SONG

After such painstaking study of empty-gate dharma,
everything life plants in the mind has dissolved away:

there's nothing left now but that old poetry demon.
A little wind or moon, and I'm chanting an idle song.

[DH]

EVENING RAIN

An early cricket sings clear, then stops.
A lamp flickers out, then flares up again.

Outside the window, telling me evening
rain's come: a clattering in banana trees.

[DH]

AUTUMN POOL

My body's idle, doing perfectly nothing,
and mind, thinking perfectly nothing,

now more than ever. In this old garden
tonight, I've returned to my autumn pool,

shoreline dark now birds have settled in,
bridge incandescent under a rising moon.

Chestnut scents swell, adrift on a breeze,
and the cinnamon's a confusion of lit dew.

So much solitude in this far end of quiet,
an isolate mystery no one finally knows:

just a few words haunting a far-off mind,
asking why it took so long coming here.

[DH]

FLOWER NO FLOWER

Flower no flower
mist no mist

arrives at midnight
and leaves at dawn

arrives like a spring dream—how many times
leaves like a morning cloud—nowhere to find.

[DH]

FOR THE BEACH GULLS

The crush of age is turning my hair white
and I'm stuck with purple robes of office,

but if my body's tangled in these fetters,
my heart abides where nothing's begun.

Happening on wine, I'm drunk in no time,
and loving those mountains, I return late.

They don't know who I am. Seeing official
falcon-banners flutter, beach gulls scatter.

[DH]

LONG LINES SENT TO LING HU-CH'U BEFORE HE COMES
TO VISIT MY TUMBLEDOWN HOME

No esteem for the stately caps and carriages of consequence,
in love with woods and streams, I go out and doze, perhaps,

drunk beside the pond. I've stopped trying to save the world,
just wander herb paths, keep my little fishing boat swept out.

Serving the poetry master with writing-brush and inkstone,
I'm steadied by music and my friend, the immortality in wine,

but for lofty sentiments, I stay close to things themselves:
green moss, rock bamboo-shoots, water lilies in white bloom.

[DH]

from WAVES SIFTING SAND

1

One anchorage of sand appears as another dissolves away,
and one fold of wave ends as another rises. Wave and sand

mingling together day after day, sifting through each other
without cease: they level up mountains and seas in no time.

2

White waves swell through wide open seas, boundless and beyond,
and level sands stretch into the four directions all endless depths:

evenings they dissolve and mornings reappear, sifting ever away,
their seasons transforming eastern seas into a field of mulberries.

3

Ten thousand miles across a lake where the grass never fades,
a lone traveler, you find yourself in rain among yellow plums,

gazing grief-stricken toward an anchorage of sand. Dark waves
wind keeps churned up: the sound of them slapping at the boat.

[DH]

OLD, AND A FEVER

I eat up, the hundred feelings vanish,
sip wine, ten thousand worries end,

and knowing we're all ravaged by age
I've grown old without all that worry.

Scholars devoting themselves to office,
farmers struggling out in their fields:

how many escape the fevers of grief?
But having only a fever of the body,

I can lie in wind at the north window
or sit beside south pond in moonlight,

take off my crow cap, sun a cold head,
or bathe feverish feet in clear water.

Passing lazy days propped on pillows,
I rise late, drift nights away in a boat,

come into all this contentment simply
because I've stopped longing for more.

Ask friends and family about Chü-i,
ask if it's true or not. They'll tell you.

But I'm still not free of words, these
lines full of heaven vast and distant,

vast and distant beyond your knowing
here in such depths of isolate mystery.

That's my fear: you might understand
and hurry here to wander beside me.

[DH]

WIND SICKNESS STRIKES

I'm 68 now, feeble and frail, besieged
feeble and frail by a hundred diseases,

but a rotting tree never avoids grubs,
and wind finds empty hollows with ease.

Fingers may be numb as willow shoots,
head tumbling, dizzy as brambleblow,

but there's this place, dead-still serene,
this heart gone blank and white as sky.

[DH]

SICK AND OLD, SAME AS EVER:
A POEM TO FIGURE IT ALL OUT

Splendor and ruin, sorrow and joy, long life or early death:
when this human realm's a figment of prank and whimsy,

is it really so strange if I'm soon a bug's arm or rat's liver?
And chicken skin or crane plumage—what would it hurt?

In yesterday's winds, I was happy to begin my long journey,
but today, in all this sunlit warmth of spring, I feel better.

And now that I'm packed and ready for that distant voyage,
what does it matter if I linger on a little while longer here?

[DH]

(I)

A thousand mountains without a bird.
Ten thousand miles with no trace of man.
A boat. An old man in a straw raincoat,
Alone in the snow, fishing in the freezing river.

[KR]

(II)
RIVER SNOW

These thousand peaks cut off the flight of birds
On all the trails, human tracks are gone.
A single boat—coat—hat—an old man!
Alone   fishing   chill   river   snow.

[GS]

(III)
RIVER SNOW

A thousand peaks: no more birds in flight.
Ten thousand paths: all trace of people gone.

In a lone boat, rain cloak and hat of reeds,
an old man's fishing the cold river snow.

[DH]

CHIA TAO

A SICK CICADA

Flight impossible, a sick cicada
comes crawling up into my hand,

broken wings still thin crystal,
bitter call still clarity perfected.

Your belly blossoms dewdrop ice
and flecks of dust clot your eyes:

you're in a bad way. And hungry
orioles and kites intend the worst.

[DH]

UNSENT

Distant clouds, trees deep into mist,
autumn bathed in a river's clarity.

Where is she tonight, so beautiful?
Moonlight floods the mountaintops.

[DH]

LI YÜ

BELLA DONNA IU

Spring flowers, autumn moon—when will you end?
How much of the past do you recall?
At the pavilion last night the east wind sobbed.
I can hardly turn my head homeward
                    in this moonlight.

The carved pillars and the jade steps are still here.
But the color of your cheeks is gone.
When asked: "How much sorrow do you still have?"
"Just like the flood of spring water
                    rushing eastward."

                                        [WCW]

Silently I ascend the western pavilion.
The moon hangs like a hairpin.
In the deep autumn garden
                    The wu-t'ung stands alone.
Involute,
Entangled,
The feeling of departure
                    Clings like a wet leaf to my heart.

                                        [WCW]

SUNG POETS

(960–1279)

AN EXCUSE FOR NOT RETURNING THE VISIT
OF A FRIEND

Do not be offended because
I am slow to go out. You know
Me too well for that. On my lap
I hold my little girl. At my
Knees stands my handsome little son.
One has just begun to talk.
The other chatters without
Stopping. They hang on my clothes
And follow my every step.
I can't get any farther
Than the door. I am afraid
I will never make it to your house.

[KR]

NEXT DOOR

My neighbors on the right
Have a young son who has just
Commenced to step out.
My neighbors on the left
Have a young daughter
Who is still a virgin.
In the heavy shadow
Under the gate it is very dark
After the sun has set.
Whose head is that, looking over the wall?

[KR]

THE CRESCENT MOON

The crescent moon shines
Over the corner of my house.
My neighbor's dogs howl.
The family is in trouble.
In the middle of the night
Spirits fly about and strange creatures stir.
A murmur runs over the high grass
Although no wind blows.

[KR]

MELON GIRL

The girl who sells melons beside the stream
Gathers her melons in the fields on the hillsides.
She does not need to spin hemp.
She has handsfull of bronze money.

[KR]

I REMEMBER THE BLUE RIVER

The moon has a halo, there will be wind.
The boatmen talk together in the night.
Dawn, a brisk wind fills our sail.
We leave the bank and speed over the white waves.
It is no use for me to be here in the land of Wu.
My dream and my desire are back in Ch'ou.
I dreamt that one day she would come with me
On a trip like this, and now she is only dust.

[KR]

READING THE POEMS OF AN ABSENT FRIEND

Tsu Mei is early dead. Chang Yu
Now is somewhere in the South.
And I, unhappy, am like
A four horse chariot which
Has lost the horses on right
And left. Their memory, like
A strong enemy, attacks
And overthrows me. The feeble
Swarm of my own thoughts struggles
In vain against the shock. All
Men respect hard work, but in
Leisure and repose they find
Happiness and peace. And me,
What is the matter with me?
Nothing, except that I cannot
Bear the loss of friends. It has
Been a long time since I have
Written a poem. My ideas
Are like sticky pudding. When
Good land is not cultivated
Regularly the grass vanishes
And is replaced by weeds, hard
To hoe. When you do not use
A well every day the pure
Water does not replace itself.
By chance, I opened a book
Of Mei's and I forgot
Everything else while the sun
Sank below the eaves. The joys
Of poetry, for those who
Appreciate them, increase with
Time and familiarity,
Their richness never ends in
Satiety. I am sorry

For the men of these times. They
Talk of nothing interesting
And have no ambition and
Die without ever being
Aware of the music of verse.
But I who am lucky enough
To appreciate these pleasures,
The more I savour, the deeper
I understand, the more I want.
In the leisure which my duties
Leave me, I stay at home, so
I can enjoy them undisturbed.
And I wonder that my feeble
Means have enabled me to
Enjoy these poems so much, that here
I have run off, like a horse
Whose rider has lost the bit.

[KR]

EAST WIND

The burgeoning trees are thick with leaves.
The birds are singing on all the hills.
The east wind blows softly.
The birds sing, the flowers dance.
This minor magistrate is drunk.
Tomorrow when he wakes up,
Spring will no longer be new.

[KR]

GREEN JADE PLUM TREES IN SPRING

Spring comes early to the gardens
Of the South, with dancing flowers.
The gentle breeze carries the sound
Of horses whinnying. The blue
Green plums are already as large
As beans. The willow leaves are long,
And really are curved like a girl's
Eyebrows. Butterflies whirl in the
Long sunlight. In the evening the
Mist lies heavy on the flowers.
The grass is covered with dew.
Girls in their transparent dresses,
Indolent and lascivious,
Lounge in their hammocks. Swallows, two
By two, nest under the painted eaves.

[KR]

OLD AGE

In the Springtime I am always
Sorry the nights are so short.
My lamp is burning out, the flame
Is low. Flying insects circle
About it. I am sick. My eyes
Are dry and dull. If I sit
Too long in one position,
All my bones ache. Chance thoughts from
I don't know where crowd upon me.
When I get to the end of a
Train of thought, I have forgotten
The beginning. For one thing
I retain I forget ten.
When I was young I liked to read.
Now I am too old to make
The effort. Then, too, if I come
Across something interesting
I have no one to talk to
About it. Sad and alone,
I sigh with self pity.

[KR]

THE RED CLIFF

The River flows to the East.
Its waves have washed away all
The heroes of history.
To the West of the ancient
Wall you enter the Red Gorge
Of Chu Ko Liang of the
Days of the Three Kingdoms. The
Jagged peaks pierce the heavens.
The furious rapids beat
At the boat, and dash up in
A thousand clouds of spray like
Snow. Mountain and river have
Often been painted, in the
Memory of the heroes
Of those days. I remember
Long ago, Kung Ch'in newly
Married to the beautiful
Chiao-siao, shining in splendor,
A young warrior, and the other
Chu Ko Liang, in his blue cap,
Waving his horsetail duster,
Smiling and chatting as he
Burned the navy of Ts'ao Ts'ao.
Their ashes were scattered to
The four winds. They vanished away
In smoke. I like to dream of
Those dead kingdoms. Let people
Laugh at my prematurely
Grey hair. My answer is
A wine cup, full of the
Moon drowned in the River.

[KR]

AT GOLD HILL MONASTERY

My native land is up there,
Far away, near the head of
The river. Just a wandering
Bureaucrat, I have been sent
To the spot where the river
Enters the sea. I have heard
That here, ten feet deep in the
Salt marsh, you can find traces
Of the sand, still cold, which bubbled
Up in the Chong Ling spring high
In the rocky plateau by
The Southern Trail. I have come
Here, following the currents
And waves. Now, high in the tower,
I overlook the whole countryside.
South of the river, north of
The river, the blue mountains
Are without number. The beauty
Of the evening cannot
Overcome my sorrow. I
Reenter my rowboat to
Return. The monks, in their lonely
Monastery, sit watching
The setting sun. The gentle breeze,
Over ten thousand acres,
Makes a fine brocade of the
Waters. In the last rays of
The twilight the schools of fish
Flicker in the water.
At this moment, out of the
River, the material
Soul of the moon is born.
Later, after the second
Watch, after the moon has set,
The heavens are left in profound
Blackness. Then in the heart of
The river, the basket torches

Of the fishermen gleam. Their
Lights come and go, shining against
The sky, and frightening the birds
Asleep on the water. I
Try to sleep, but my heart is
Troubled, my mind is distracted.
Neither men nor ghosts come here.
What is it then? Has the spirit
Of the river shown me a
Vision to warn me? Since the
River mouth and the islands
Affect me so, I will not come
Again to this monastery.
I thank the spirit of the river,
But what good has it done?
Just as its waters cannot
Return to their source, so I can
Never return to my native land.

[KR]

THE SOUTHERN ROOM OVER THE RIVER

The room is prepared, the incense burned.
I close the shutters before I close my eyelids.
The patterns of the quilt repeat the waves of the river.
The gauze curtain is like a mist.
Then a dream comes to me and when I awake
I no longer know where I am.
I open the western window and watch the waves
Stretching on and on to the horizon.

[KR]

The spring wind raises fine dust from the road.
Everybody is out, enjoying the new leaves.
Strollers are drinking in the inns along the way.
Cart wheels roll over the young grass.
The whole town has gone to the suburbs.
Children scamper everywhere and shout to the skies.
Songs and drum beats scare the hills
And make the leaves tremble on the trees.
Picnic baskets and jugs litter the fields
And put the crows and kites to flight.
Who is that fellow who has gathered a crowd?
He says he is a Taoist monk.
He is selling charms to the passersby.
He shouts, waves his hands, rolls his eyes.
"If you raise silk, these will
Grow cocoons as big as pitchers.
If you raise stock, these will
Make the sheep as big as elks."
Nobody really believes him.
It is the spirit of spring in him they are buying.
As soon as he has enough money
He will go fill himself with wine
And fall down drunk,
Overcome by the magic of his own charms.

[KR]

In the golden twilight the rain
Was like silk threads. During the night
It cleared. The wind fell. It grew
Colder. My covers felt damp
And cold. Without my knowing it,
The snow had drifted into
The room like heaps of salt. At
The fifth watch, in the first flush
Of dawn, I close the curtain
Of the study. During the
Rest of the night I listen
To the ice, warping the colored
Tiles of the roof. In the morning
I sweep the Northern terrace
And look out at Saddle Peak.
It is clear of clouds and I
Can see both summits. Above
The village in the morning
Sunlight, crows begin to circle.
The mud of the streets is covered
With white. No cart track has marked it.
Ice has turned the shop roofs to
White jade. Snow has filled the doorways
With rice. The last cicadas
Have long since gone to earth. Now
They will have to dig a thousand
Feet deeper. Some clouds pile up,
The color of dried moss. My
Chest bothers me again.
I feel I have lost the
Ability to write.
The icicles on the eaves
Drone in the wind like the swords
Of murderers.

[KR]

THE TURNING YEAR

Nightfall. Clouds scatter and vanish.
The sky is pure and cold.
Silently the River of Heaven turns in the Jade Vault.
If tonight I do not enjoy life to the full,
Next month, next year, who knows where I will be?

[KR]

EPIGRAM

I fish for minnows in the lake.
Just born, they have no fear of man.
And those who have learned,
Never come back to warn them.

[KR]

RAIN IN THE ASPENS

My neighbor to the East has
A grove of aspens. Tonight
The rain sounds mournfully in
Them. Alone, at my window,
I cannot sleep. Autumn insects
Swarm, attracted by my light.

[KR]

TO A TRAVELER

Last year when I accompanied you
As far as the Yang Chou Gate,
The snow was flying, like white willow cotton.
This year, Spring has come again,
And the willow cotton is like snow.
But you have not come back.
Alone before the open window,
I raise my wine cup to the shining moon.
The wind, moist with evening dew,
Blows the gauze curtains.
Maybe Chang-O the moon goddess,
Will pity this single swallow
And join us together with the cord of light
That reaches beneath the painted eaves of your home.

[KR]

REMEMBERING MIN CH'E
A LETTER TO HIS BROTHER SU CHE

What is our life on earth?
A flock of migrating geese
Rest for a moment on the snow,
Leave the print of their claws
And fly away, some East, some West.
The old monk is no more.
There is a new gravestone for him.
On the broken wall of his hut
You can't find the poems we wrote.
There's nothing to show we've ever been there.
The road was long. We were tired out.
My limping mule brayed all the way.

[KR]

THOUGHTS IN EXILE

I lift my head and watch
The phoenix and the snowy swan
Cross the heavens in their migrations.
Wealth, office, position,
After all these years, mean nothing to me.
The foundered horse no longer
Hopes to travel a thousand miles.
In exile, in autumn,
I grow lazy and indifferent.
In history men have
Always been treated like this.
I am forbidden to visit the Western Lake.
There is no place else I want to go.
The wise man, no matter how he is treated,
Knows that Heaven does nothing without reason.
But nobody can stop me
From writing poems about the
Mountains and rivers of Wu.

[KR]

SORROW

The white moon gleams through scudding
Clouds in the cold sky of the Ninth
Month. The white frost weighs down the
Leaves and the branches bend low
Over the freezing water.
All alone I sit by my
Window. The crushing burden
Of the passing days never
Grows lighter for an instant.
I write poems, change and correct them,
And finally throw them away.
Gold chrysanthemums wither
Along the balcony. Hard
Cries of migrating storks fall
Heavily from the icy sky.
All alone by my window
Hidden in my empty room,
All alone, I burn incense,
And dream in the smoke, all alone.

[KR]

SPRING JOY

Drafty winds and fine rain
Make a chilly Spring.
I drink wine, remembering bygone happiness,
Under the pear blossoms,
Weeping with misery.
Through the scented grasses
And broken mists, we walked
Along the Southern bank of the river,
Tears of farewell
Blurring the distant mountains.
Last night I was fulfilled in a dream.
Speechless, we made love
In mist and clouds.
Alas, when I awoke
The old agony returned.
I tossed in my quilt
Angry at my own helplessness.
It is easier to see Heaven
Than to see you.

[KR]

SPRING NIGHT
TO THE TUNE "PANNING GOLD"

My jade body, like my gold hairpins,
Is still as lovely as it was that evening
When for the first time,
You turned me away from the lamplight
And unfastened the belt
Of my embroidered skirt.
Now our quilts and pillows are cold,
And the incense of that evening has long faded.
Behind the closed doors of the deep courtyard
Spring is silent and lonely.
Flowers fall with the rain, all the long night.
Agony mingles with my dreams
And makes me still more helpless
And hopeless.

[KR]

PLAINT

Spring flowers, Autumn moons,
Water lilies still carry
Away my heart like a lost
Boat. As long as I am flesh
And bone I will never find
Rest. There will never come a
Time when I will be able
To resist my emotions.

[KR]

SORROW OF DEPARTURE
TO THE TUNE "CUTTING A FLOWERING PLUM BRANCH"

Red lotus incense fades on
The jeweled curtain. Autumn
Comes again. Gently I open
My silk dress and float alone
On the orchid boat. Who can
Take a letter beyond the clouds?
Only the wild geese come back
And write their ideograms
On the sky under the full
Moon that floods the West Chamber.
Flowers, after their kind, flutter
And scatter. Water after
Its nature, when spilt, at last
Gathers again in one place.
Creatures of the same species
Long for each other. But we
Are far apart and I have
Grown learned in sorrow.
Nothing can make it dissolve
And go away. One moment,
It is on my eyebrows.
The next it weighs on my heart.

[KR]

FADING PLUM BLOSSOMS
TO THE TUNE "PERFUMED GARDEN"

Spring is hidden in my studio,
Daylight locked out of my window.
My painted room is profoundly secluded.
The seal character incense is burned out.
The shadows of the sunset
Descend across the curtain hooks.
Now that the wild plum I planted myself
Is blooming so well this year
I do not need to climb the waterfall
Seeking wild plum blossoms.
No one comes to visit me.
I am as lonely as ever was Ho Sun in Yang Chou.
I know that although my plum blossoms
Are lovelier than all others
The rain will soon scatter them in disorder,
And the wind pluck them away.
The sound of a horizontal flute fills the whole house
With a melody of dense sorrow.
I will not feel badly when their perfume dissolves
And their jade snow petals fall.
When they have all been swept away
The memory of my love for them will remain.
It is difficult to describe the beauty of their shadows
Cast by the pale moonlight.

[KR]

AUTUMN LOVE

"A WEARY SONG TO A SLOW SAD TUNE"

Search. Search. Seek. Seek.
Cold. Cold. Clear. Clear.
Sorrow. Sorrow. Pain. Pain.
Hot flashes. Sudden chills.
Stabbing pains. Slow agonies.
I can find no peace.
I drink two cups, then three bowls
Of clear wine until I can't
Stand up against a gust of wind.
Wild geese fly overhead.
They wrench my heart.
They were our friends in the old days.
Gold chrysanthemums litter
The ground, pile up, faded, dead.
This season I could not bear
To pick them. All alone,
Motionless at my window,
I watch the gathering shadows.
Fine rain sifts through the wu-t'ung trees.
And drips, drop by drop, through the dusk.
What can I ever do now?
How can I drive off this word—
Hopelessness?

[KR]

TO THE TUNE "THE BODHISATTVA'S HEADDRESS"

Breeze soft, sun frail, spring still early.
In a new lined dress my heart was refreshed,
But when I rose from sleep I felt a chill.
I put plum blossoms in my hair.
Now they are withered.
Where is my homeland?
I forget it only when drunk.
The sandalwood incense burned out while I slept.
Now the perfume has gone,
But the wine has not gone.

[KR]

BANANA TREES
TO THE TUNE "PICKING MULBERRIES"

Who planted banana trees in front of my window?
Their shadows fall in the midst of the courtyard.
Their shadows fall in the midst of the courtyard.
Leaves like hearts, leaves like hearts,
That open and close with excess of love.
Midnight, rain on the leaves saddens my own heart.
Dien! Di! Dien! Di! Bitter cold, unceasing rain.
Drip! Drop! Drip! Drop! Bitter cold, unceasing rain.
Loneliness. Loneliness.
Sorrow corrodes this exile from the North.
How can I bear to lie awake and listen?

[KR]

The sky turns,
The Autumn light turns,
And my heart aches.
I visit the golden flowers
And realize that the Ninth Day of the Ninth Month
Will soon be here.
I try on a new dress
And taste the new green thick wine.
By turns the weather is windy, rainy, and chilly.
As the orange twilight fills the courtyard
I am overwhelmed with anxiety.
The wine awakens all the sorrow of the past in my breast.
How can I bear the endless night,
The full moon's light on our empty bed,
The sound of the fullers' mallets,
Beating cloth for winter,
The shrill crying of the crickets,
And the lingering notes of the bugles?

[KR]

ON SPRING

TO THE TUNE "THE SILK WASHING BROOK"

I idle at the window
In the small garden.
The Spring colors are bright.
Inside, the curtains have not been raised
And the room is deep in shadow.
In my high chamber
I silently play my jade zither.
Far-off mountain caves spit clouds,
Hastening the coming of dusk.
A light breeze brings puffs of rain
And casts moving shadows on the ground.
I am afraid I cannot keep
The pear blossoms from withering.

[KR]

SPRING FADES

Spring fades. Why should I suffer so much from homesickness?
I am ill. Combing my long hair exasperates me.
Under the roof beams the swallows chatter too much all day long.
A soft breeze fills the curtains with the perfume of roses.

[KR]

A SONG OF DEPARTURE
TO THE TUNE "BUTTERFLIES LOVE FLOWERS"

Warm rain and soft breeze by turns
Have just broken
And driven away the chill.
Moist as the pussy willows,
Light as the plum blossoms,
Already I feel the heart of Spring vibrating.
But now who will share with me
The joys of wine and poetry?
Tears streak my rouge.
My hairpins are too heavy.
I put on my new quilted robe
Sewn with gold thread
And throw myself against a pile of pillows,
Crushing my phoenix hairpins.
Alone, all I can embrace is my endless sorrow.
I know a good dream will never come.
So I stay up till past midnight
Trimming the lamp flower's smoking wick.

[KR]

SPRING ENDS
TO THE TUNE "SPRING AT WU LING"

The gentle breeze has died down.
The perfumed dust has settled.
It is the end of the time
Of flowers. Evening falls
And all day I have been too
Lazy to comb my hair.
Our furniture is just the same.
He no longer exists.
All effort would be wasted.
Before I can speak,
My tears choke me.
I hear that Spring at Two Rivers
Is still beautiful.
I had hoped to take a boat there,
But I know so fragile a vessel
Won't bear such a weight of sorrow.

[KR]

WRITTEN BY CHANCE

Fifteen years ago, beneath moonlight and flowers,
I walked with you
We composed flower-viewing poems together.
Tonight the moonlight and flowers are just the same
But how can I ever hold in my arms the same love.

[KR]

WRITTEN ON THE SEVENTH DAY OF THE SEVENTH MONTH
TO THE TUNE "YOU MOVE IN FRAGRANCE"

Deep in the grass the crickets sing.
Wu-t'ung leaves fall suddenly and startle me.
Sorrow lies thick
On the ways of men and high Heaven.
On the cloud stairs to the floor of moonlight
The doors are all locked for a thousand miles.
Even if our floating rafts could come and go
We could not meet each other,
Nor cross the star bridge of magpies.
Once a year the Cowboy and Weaving Girl meet.
Imagine the year-long bitterness of their parting.
Now suddenly in the midst of their love-making
The wind blows first clear and then rain.

[KR]

Year after year in the snow, intoxicated,
I have put the new plum blossoms
In my hair.
Now the fallen petals
Only depress me.
All I have gained is a dress
Wet with crystal tears.
This year I am at the corner
Of the sea and the edge of Heaven.
I am old and lonely.
My temples have turned white.
I realize that the evening wind
Is too strong for me.
It is no longer possible
For me to contemplate
The blossoming plums.

[KR]

LU YU

(I)
RAIN ON THE RIVER

In the fog we drift hither
And yon over the dark waves.
At last our little boat finds
Shelter under a willow bank.
At midnight I am awake,
Heavy with wine. The smoky
Lamp is still burning. The rain
Is still sighing in the bamboo
Thatch of the cabin of the boat.

[KR, 1956]

(II)
RAIN ON THE RIVER

We cross the river over dark waves
Through dense fog and tie up the little boat
Under the bank to a willow.
I wake up heavy with wine in the middle of the night.
The lamp is only a
Smoky red coal. I lie listening to the
Hsiao hsiao of the rain on the bamboo roof
Of the cabin.

[KR, 1970]

I

IDLENESS

I keep the rustic gate closed
For fear somebody might step
On the green moss. The sun grows
Warmer. You can tell it's Spring.
Once in a while, when the breeze
Shifts, I can hear the sounds of the
Village. My wife is reading
The classics. Now and then she
Asks me the meaning of a word.
I call for wine and my son
Fills my cup till it runs over.
I have only a little
Garden, but it is planted
With yellow and purple plums.

[KR, 1956]

(II)

LAZY

Once we had a knocker
On the gate.
Now we seldom
Open it. I don't want people
Scuffing up the green moss.
The sun grows warm. Spring has really
Come at last. Sometimes you
Can hear faintly on the gentle
Breeze the noise of the street.
My wife is reading the classics.
She asks me the meaning
Of ancient characters.
My son begs for a sip of wine.
He drinks the whole cup before
I can stop him.

Is there anything
Better than an enclosed garden
With yellow plums and purple plums
Planted alternately?

[KR, 1970]

(I)
NIGHT THOUGHTS

I cannot sleep. The long, long
Night is full of bitterness.
I sit alone in my room,
Beside a smoky lamp.
I rub my heavy eyelids
And idly turn the pages
Of my book. Again and again
I trim my brush and stir the ink.
The hours go by. The moon comes
In the open window, pale
And bright like new money.
At last I fall asleep and
I dream of the days on the
River at Tsa-feng, and the
Friends of my youth in Yen Chao.
Young and happy we ran
Over the beautiful hills.
And now the years have gone by,
And I have never gone back.

[KR, 1956]

II

INSOMNIA

Even when I fall asleep early,
My nights are long and full of bitterness.
Tonight, tortured with insomnia,
Memories of the past flood back
Until they have exhausted me.
Alone in the house beside a smoky lamp,
I rub my heavy eyelids
And idly turn the pages of my notebook.
Again and again I scratch my head
And trim my brush and stir the heavy ink.
The hours go by. The moon comes
And stands in the open door,
White and shining like molten silver.
Suddenly I am back, sailing on Ts'ai Fong River
With the fellows of my youth,
Back in Yuen village.
Oh wonderful mountains! Oh noble boys!
How is it that I have lived so long
And never once gone back to visit you?

[KR, 1970]

THE WILD FLOWER MAN

Do you know the old man who
Sells flowers by the South Gate?
He lives on flowers like a bee.
In the morning he sells mallows,
In the evening he has poppies.
His shanty roof lets in the
Blue sky. His rice bin is
Always empty. When he has
Made enough money from his
Flowers, he heads for a teahouse.
When his money is gone, he
Gathers some more flowers.
All the spring weather, while the
Flowers are in bloom, he is
In bloom, too. Every day he
Is drunk all day long. What does
He care if new laws are posted
At the Emperor's palace?
What does it matter to him
If the government is built
On sand? If you try to talk
To him, he won't answer but
Only give you a drunken
Smile from under his tousled hair.

[KR]

A COLD FLY

Chance sight on a windowsill, the fly sits warming its back,
rubbing its front legs together, savoring morning sunlight.

Sun nudges shadow closer. But the fly knows what's coming,
and suddenly it's gone—a buzz heading for the next window.

[DH]

COLD SPARROWS

A hundred thousand sparrows descend on my empty courtyard.
A few gather atop the plums, chatting with clear evening skies,

and the rest swarm around, trying to kill me with their racket.
Suddenly they all startle away, and there's silence: not a sound.

[DH]

NIGHT RAIN AT LUSTER GAP

The gorge's river all empty clarity, rain sweeps in,
cold breezy whispers beginning deep in the night,

and ten thousand pearls start clattering on a plate,
each one's *tic* a perfect clarity piercing my bones.

I scratch my head in dream, then get up and listen
till dawn, hearing each sound appear and disappear.

I've listened to rain all my life. My hair's white now,
and I still don't know night rain on a spring river.

[DH]

TO AN OLD TUNE

In my young days I never
Tasted sorrow. I wanted
To become a famous poet.
I wanted to get ahead
So I pretended to be sad.
Now I am old and have known
The depths of every sorrow,
And I am content to loaf
And enjoy the clear Autumn.

[KR]

CHIANG CHIEH

TO THE TUNE "THE FAIR MAID OF YU"

Once when young I lay and listened
To the rain falling on the roof
Of a brothel. The candle light
Gleamed on silk and silky flesh.
Later I heard it on the
Cabin roof of a small boat
On the Great River, under
Low clouds, where wild geese cried out
On the Autumn storm. Now I
Hear it again on the monastery
Roof. My hair has turned white.
Joy—sorrow—parting—meeting—
Are all as though they had
Never been. Only the rain
Is the same, falling in streams
On the tiles, all through the night.

[KR]

ON CHINESE POETRY

RHYMEPROSE ON LITERATURE

TRANSLATED BY ACHILLES FANG

PREFACE

Whenever I study the works of gifted writers I flatter myself that I know how their minds moved.

Certainly expression in language and the charging of words with meaning can be done variously.

And yet beauty and ugliness, good and bad can be distinguished.

By writing again and again myself, I obtain more and more insight.

My worry is that my ideas may not equal their subjects and my style may fall short of my ideas.

The difficulty, then, lies not so much in the knowing as in the doing.

I have written this rhymeprose on literature to tell of the consummate art of past writers and to present the why and how of good and bad writing as well.

I hope it will prove in time to be a comprehensive essay.

Surely, hewing an ax handle with a handle in hand, the pattern should not be far to seek.

However, as each artist has his own way to magic, I despair of doing him justice.

Nevertheless, whatever I can say I have set down here.

PREPARATION

Standing at the center of things, the poet contemplates the enigma of the universe; he nourishes his feelings and his intellect on the great works of the past.

Concurring with the four seasons, he sighs at the passage of time; gazing at the myriad things, he thinks of the world's complexity.

He grieves for the falling leaves of lusty autumn; he rejoices in the frail bud of fragrant spring.

He senses awe in his heart as at the touch of frost; his spirit reaches for the vast as he lifts his eyes to the clouds.

He chants the splendid achievement of his forebears; he sings the clean fragrance of his predecessors.

He wanders in the forest of letters, and hymns the order of great art.

Moved, he puts his books aside and takes the writing-brush, to express himself in letters.

PROCESS

At first, he shuts his eyes, listening inwardly; he is lost in thought, questioning everywhere.

His spirit rides to the eight ends of the universe; his mind travels thousands of cubits up and down.

At last, his mood dawns clearer and clearer; objects, clear-limned, push one another forth.

He pours out the essence of letters; he savors the extract of the six arts.

He floats on the heavenly lake; he steeps himself in the nether spring.

Thereupon, submerged words squirm up, as when a flashing fish, hook in its gills, leaps from water's depth; hovering beauties flutter down, as when a soaring bird, harpoon-string about its wings, falls from a crest of cloud.

He gathers words untouched by a hundred generations; he plucks rhythms unsung for a thousand years.

He spurns the morning blossom, now full blown; he spreads the evening bud, yet unopen.

He sees past and present in a moment; he reaches for the four seas in the twinkling of an eye.

WORDS, WORDS, WORDS

Now, he selects his ideas and puts them in order; he examines his words and fits them into place.

He sounds all that is colorful; he twangs everything that rings.

Often he shakes the foliage by tugging the twig; often he traces the current to the source.

Sometimes he brings to light what was hidden; sometimes he traps a hard prey while seeking an easy one.

Now the tiger puts on new stripes, to the consternation of other beasts; now the dragon emerges, and terrifies all the birds.

Maybe things fit, are easy to manage; maybe they jar, are awkward to manipulate.

He empties his mind completely to concentrate his thoughts; he collects his
wits before he puts words together.

He traps heaven and earth in the cage of form; he crushes the myriad things at
the tip of his brush.

At first they hesitate upon his parched lips; at last they flow from his deep-
dipped brush.

Reason, supporting the substances, bolsters the trunk; style, hanging from it,
spreads luxuriance.

Emotion and expression are never at odds: all changes in his mood are exposed
on his face.

If the thought impinges on joy, a smile is ineluctable; no sooner does grief find
words than a sigh escapes.

Sometimes words flow easily as soon as he holds the brush; sometimes he sits
vacantly, nibbling on it.

THE PLEASURE OF WRITING

There is joy in this vocation; all sages esteem it.

We wrestle with non-being to force it into being; we beat silence for an answer-
ing music.

We lock a whole infinity in a square foot of silk; we pour a deluge from the
inch-space of the heart.

Language spreads wider and wider; thoughts probe deeper and deeper.

The scent of sweet blossom is diffused; the thrust of green twigs is budding.

Laughing wind will fly and whirl upward; pregnant clouds will arise from the
forest of writing-brushes.

GENRES

Figures vary in a thousand ways; things are not of one measure.

Confusing and fleeting, shapes are hard to capture.

Words vie with words for mastery, but it is mind that disposes them.

Faced with creating something or leaving it unborn, he groans; caught between
light touch and deep incision, he chooses boldly.

He may depart from the square and deviate from the compasses; for he is bent
on exploring the shape and exhausting the reality.

And so, he who would dazzle the eyes exploits splendor; he who intends to sat-
isfy the mind values cogency.

He whose reasoning is rarefied should not be fettered by details; he whose dis-
course is noble may unbind his language.

. . . .

Shih (lyric poetry) traces emotions daintily; *Fu* (rhymeprose) depicts things brightly.

Pei (epitaph) balances facts with fancy; *Lei* (dirge) is gripping and mournful; *Chen* (admonition) praises or blames, is clear-cut and nervous.

Sung (eulogy) is natural and free, rich and full; *Lun* (disquisition) is compact and subtle, bright and smooth.

Tsou (memorial to the throne) is quiet and penetrating, genteel and decorous; *Shuo* (discourse) is dazzling and extravagant.

Different as these forms are, they all shun depravity and interdict license.

Essentially, language must communicate, and reason must dominate; prolixity and verbosity are not commended.

THE MUSIC OF POETRY

Literature is a thing that assumes various shapes and undergoes many changes in form.

Ideas should be skillfully brought together; language should be beautifully expressed.

The mutation of sounds and tones should be like the five colors of embroidery sustaining each other.

True, moods come and go, and embarrass us by their capriciousness.

But if we can rise to all emergencies and know the correct order, it will be like opening a channel from a spring.

If, however, proper juxtaposition is not made at the proper point, we will be putting the tail at the head.

The sequence of azure and yellow being disturbed, the color scheme will be blurred and vague.

THE ART OF REWRITING

Now you glance back and are constrained by an earlier line; now you look ahead and are coerced by the anticipated passage.

Sometimes your words jar though your reasoning is clear; sometimes your language is smooth while your ideas are lame.

Such collisions avoided, both will gain; forced together, both will suffer.

Weigh merit or demerit by the milligram; decide rejection or retention by a hairbreadth.

If your idea or word has not the correct weight, it has to go, however comely it may look.

KEY PASSAGES

It may be that your language is ample and your reasoning rich, yet your ideas
do not round out.

If what must go on cannot be ended, what has been said in full cannot be added
to.

Put down terse phrases at key positions; they will invigorate the whole piece.

Your words will acquire their intended values in the light of such phrases.

This useful device will spare you the pain of deleting and excising.

ORIGINALITY

It may be that language and thought blend into perfect tapestry—fresh, gay,
and exuberantly lush,

Flaming like many-colored broidery, mournful as multiple chords;

But there is nothing novel in my thinking, if it tallies with earlier masterpieces.

True, the shuttle has plied my heart; what a pity, that others preceded.

As my integrity would be impaired and my probity damaged, I must renounce
the piece, however proud I am of it.

PURPLE PATCHES

Perhaps one ear of the stalk has opened, its tip prominent, solitary, and unsur-
passingly exquisite.

But shadows cannot be caught; echoes are hard to hold.

Standing forlorn, your purple passage juts out; it can't be woven into ordinary
music.

Your mind, out of step, finds no mate for it; your spirit, desperately wandering,
will not surrender it.

When the rock embeds jade, the mountain glows; when the stream is impreg-
nated with pearls, the river becomes alluring.

When the arrow-thorn bush is spared from the sickle, it will glory in its foliage.

Let's weave the market ditty into the classical melody; perhaps we may hold on
to what we find beautiful.

FIVE CRITERIA

Music

Perhaps you are toying with anemic rhythms: living in a desert, you only amuse
yourself.

When you look down into silence, you see no friend; when you lift your gaze
   to space, you hear no echo.
It is like striking a single chord—it rings out, but there is no music.

Harmony

Perhaps you fit your words to a feeble music; merely gaudy, your language is
   not charming.
As beauty and ugliness are commingled, what is good suffers.
Like the harsh note of a wind instrument below in the court-yard, there is
   music but no harmony.

Sadness

Perhaps you forsake reason to strive for novelty; you go after the inane and
   pursue the trivial.
Your language wants sincerity and is deficient in love; your words wash back
   and forth, and never come to the point.
They are like thin chords reverberating—there is harmony, but they are not sad.

Decorum

Possibly by galloping unbridled, you make your poem sound well; it is loud and
   seductive.
Merely pleasing to the eye, it mates with vulgarity—a fine voice but an unwor-
   thy song.
Like *Fang-lu* and *Sang-kien*, it is sad but not decorous.

Richness

Perhaps your poem is clean and pared, all superfluities removed.
So much so that it lacks even the lingering flavor of a sacrificial broth; it resem-
   bles the limpid tune of the vermillion chord.
One man sings, and three men carry the refrain; it is decorous, but it is not rich.

VARIABILITY

As to whether your work should be full or close-fitting, whether you should
   shape it by gazing down or looking up,
You must accommodate necessary variation, if you would bring out the latent
   qualities.
When your language is uncouth, your conceits can be clever; when your rea-
   soning is awkward, your words can be supple.

You may follow the well-worn path to attain novelty; you may wade the muddy water to reach the clear stream.

Perspicacity comes after examination; subtlety demands refining.

It is like dancers flinging their sleeves in harmony with the beat, or singers throwing their voices in tune with the chord.

All this is what the wheelwright P'ien despaired of explaining; nor can mere language describe it.

MASTERPIECES

I have been paying tribute to laws of language and rules of style.

I have come to know what the world blames, and am aware of what the masters praised.

Originality is a thing often looked at askance by the fixed eye.

Emerald and jade, they say, can be picked as so many beans in the middle of the field,

As timeless as the universe and growing co-eternally with heaven and earth.

The world may abound with gems; yet they do not fill my two hands.

THE POET'S DESPAIR

How I grieve that the bottle is often empty; how I sorrow that True Word is hard to emulate.

And so I limp along with anemic rhythms and make indifferent music to complete the song.

I always conclude a piece with lingering regret; how can I be self-satisfied?

I fear to be a drummer of an earthen jug; the players of jade instruments will laugh at me.

INSPIRATION

Flow

As for the interaction of stimulus and response, and the principle of the flowing and ebbing of inspiration,

You cannot hinder its coming or stop its going.

It vanishes like a shadow and it returns like echoes.

When the heavenly arrow is at its fleetest and sharpest, what confusion cannot be brought to order?

The wind of thought bursts from the heart; the stream of words gushes through the lips and teeth.

Luxuriance and magnificence wait the command of the brush and the silk.

Shining and glittering, language fills your eyes; abundant and overflowing, music drowns your ears.

Ebb

When the six emotions become sluggish and stagnant, the mood gone but the psyche remaining,

You will be as abject as a dead stump, as empty as the bed of a dry river.

You probe into the hidden depth of your animal soul; you spur your spirit to reveal itself.

But your reason, darkened, is crouching lower and lower; your thought must be dragged out by force, wriggling and struggling.

So it is that you make many errors by straining your emotions, and commit fewer mistakes when you let your ideas run freely.

True, the thing lies within me, but it is not in my power to force it out.

And so, time and again I beat my empty breast and groan; I really do not know the causes of the flowing and the not flowing.

CODA: THE USE OF POETRY

Literature is the embodiment of our thoughts.

It travels over endless miles, sweeping all obstructions aside; it spans innumerable years, acting as a bridge.

Looking down, it bequeaths patterns to the future; gazing up, it contemplates the examples of the ancients.

It preserves the way of Wen and Wu, about to crumble; it propagates good ethos, never to perish.

No realm is too far for it to reach; no thought is too subtle for it to comprehend.

It is the equal of clouds and rain in yielding sweet moisture; it is like spirits and ghosts in effecting metamorphoses.

It inscribes bronze and marble, to make virtue known; it breathes through flutes and strings, and is new always.

from THE CHINESE WRITTEN CHARACTER
AS A MEDIUM FOR POETRY

My subject is poetry, not language, yet the roots of poetry are in language. In the study of a language so alien in form to ours as is Chinese in its written character, it is necessary to inquire how these universal elements of form which constitute poetics can derive appropriate nutriment.

In what sense can verse, written in terms of visible hieroglyphics, be reckoned true poetry? It might seem that poetry, which like music is a *time art*, weaving its unities out of successive impressions of sound, could with difficulty assimilate a verbal medium consisting largely of semi-pictorial appeals to the eye.

Contrast, for example, Gray's line:

The curfew tolls the knell of parting day

with the Chinese line:

| Moon | Rays | Like | Pure | Snow |

Unless the sound of the latter be given, what have they in common? It is not enough to adduce that each contains a certain body of prosaic meaning; for the question is, how can the Chinese line imply, *as form*, the very element that distinguishes poetry from prose?

On second glance, it is seen that the Chinese words, though visible, occur in just as necessary an order as the phonetic symbols of Gray. All that poetic form requires is a regular and flexible sequence, as plastic as thought itself. The characters may be seen and read, silently by the eye, one after the other:

Moon rays like pure snow.

Perhaps we do not always sufficiently consider that thought is successive, not through some accident or weakness of our subjective operations but because the operations of nature are successive. The transferences of force from agent to object, which constitute natural phenomena, occupy time. Therefore, a reproduction of them in imagination requires the same temporal order.

Suppose that we look out of a window and watch a man. Suddenly he turns his head and actively fixes his attention upon something. We look ourselves and see that his vision has been focused upon a horse. We saw, first, the man before he acted; second, while he acted; third, the object toward which his action was directed. In speech we split up the rapid continuity of this action and of its picture into its three essential parts or joints in the right order, and say:

Man sees horse.

It is clear that these three joints, or words, are only three phonetic symbols, which stand for the three terms of a natural process. But we could quite as easily denote these three stages of our thought by symbols equally arbitrary, *which had no basis in sound;* for example, by three Chinese characters:

人　　　　　見　　　　　馬

Man　　　　　*Sees*　　　　　*Horse*

If we all knew *what division* of this mental horse-picture each of these signs stood for, we could communicate continuous thought to one another as easily by drawing them as by speaking words. We habitually employ the visible language of gesture in much this same manner.

But Chinese notation is something much more than arbitrary symbols. It is based upon a vivid shorthand picture of the operations of nature. In the algebraic figure and in the spoken word there is no natural connection between thing and sign: all depends upon sheer convention. But the Chinese method follows natural suggestion. First stands the man on his two legs. Second, his eye moves through space: a bold figure represented by running legs under an eye, a modified picture of an eye, a modified picture of running legs, but unforgettable once you have seen it. Third stands the horse on his four legs.

The thought-picture is not only called up by these signs as well as by words, but far more vividly and concretely. Legs belong to all three characters: they are *alive*. The group holds something of the quality of a continuous moving picture.

The untruth of a painting or a photograph is that, in spite of its concreteness, it drops the element of natural succession.

Contrast the Laocoön statue with Browning's lines:

I sprang to the stirrup, and Joris, and he

. . . . . .

And into the midnight we galloped abreast.

One superiority of verbal poetry as an art rests in its getting back to the fundamental reality of *time*. Chinese poetry has the unique advantage of combining both elements. It speaks at once with the vividness of painting, and with the mobility of sounds. It is, in some sense, more objective than either, more dramatic. In reading Chinese we do not seem to be juggling mental counters, but to be watching *things* work out their own fate.

Leaving for a moment the form of the sentence, let us look more closely at this quality of vividness in the structure of detached Chinese words. The earlier forms of these characters were pictorial, and their hold upon the imagination is little shaken, even in later conventional modifications. It is not so well known, perhaps, that the great number of these ideographic roots carry in them a *verbal idea of action*. It might be thought that a picture is naturally the picture of a *thing*, and that therefore the root ideas of Chinese are what grammar calls nouns.

But examination shows that a large number of the primitive Chinese characters, even the so-called radicals, are shorthand pictures of actions or processes.

For example, the ideograph meaning "to speak" is a mouth with two words and a flame coming out of it. The sign meaning "to grow up with difficulty" is grass with a twisted root. But this concrete *verb* quality, both in nature and in the Chinese signs, becomes far more striking and poetic when we pass from such simple, original pictures to compounds. In this process of compounding, two things added together do not produce a third thing but suggest some fundamental relation between them. For example, the ideograph for a "messmate" is a man and a fire.

A true noun, an isolated thing, does not exist in nature. Things are only the terminal points, or rather the meeting points, of actions, cross-sections cut through actions, snap-shots. Neither can a pure verb, an abstract motion, be possible in nature. The eye sees noun and verb as one: things in motion, motion in things, and so the Chinese conception tends to represent them.

The sun underlying the bursting forth of plants = spring.

The sun sign tangled in the branches of the tree sign = east.

"Rice-field" plus "struggle"= male.

"Boat" plus "water"= boat-water, a ripple.

ON REXROTH'S
ONE HUNDRED POEMS FROM THE CHINESE

Kenneth Rexroth has recently translated *One Hundred Poems from the Chinese*, one of the most brilliantly sensitive books of poems in the American idiom it has ever been my good fortune to read.

It must be amazing to the occidental reader, acquainted we'll say with Palgrave's *Golden Treasury*, to realize that the Chinese have a practice and art of the poem, which in subtlety of lyrical candor, far exceeds his own. I am grateful to him. Nothing comparable and as relaxed is to be found I think in the whole of English or American verse, and in French or Spanish verse, so far as I know. So that it constitutes a unique experience to read what has been set down here.

Womanhood has been engraved on our minds in unforgettable terms. Oh, I know that women can be bitches, you don't have to be a homosexual to learn that, but the exact and telling and penetrant realization of a woman's reality, of her lot, has never been better set down. It is tremendously moving, as none of our well-known attempts, say, throughout the Renaissance have ever succeeded in being.

This is a feat of overwhelming importance. It is not a question of a man or woman's excess in experience or suffering, for whatever this amounted to, they have had to do; but that in their mutual love they have been made to bear their fates. What does it matter what a woman and a man in love will do for themselves? Someone will succeed and someone will die. In the poem suddenly we realize that we know that and perceive in a single burst of vision, in a flash that dazzles the reader.

The poet Tu Fu (713–770) was the first, with him it begins. Homer and Sappho with their influence on our poetry had been dead for over a thousand years. The use of the metaphor, pivotal in our own day, had not been discovered by the Chinese in these ancient masterpieces. The metaphor comes as a flash, nascent in the line, which flares when the image is suddenly shifted and we are jolted awake just as when the flint strikes the steel. The same that the Chinese poet seeks more simply when the beauty of his images bursts at one stroke directly upon us.

The city is silent,
Sound drains away,
Buildings vanish in the light of dawn,
Cold sunlight comes on the highest peak,
The thick dust of night
Clings to the hills,
The earth opens,
The river boats are vague,
The still sky—
The sound of falling leaves.
A huge doe comes to the garden gate,
Lost from the herd,
Seeking its fellows.

Tu Fu

Where is the poem? without metaphor among these pages so effortlessly put down. Occidental art seems more than a little strained compared to this simplicity. You cannot say there is no art since we are overwhelmed by it. The person of the poet, the poetess, no, the woman herself (when it is a woman), speaks to us . . . in an unknown language, to our very ears, so that we actually weep with her and what she says (while we are not aware of her secret) is that she breathes . . . that she is alive as we are.

Where is it hidden in the words? Our own clumsy poems, the best of them, following the rules of grammar . . . trip themselves up. What is a sonnet of Shakespeare beside this limpidity but a gauche, a devised pretext? and it takes fourteen lines rigidly to come to its conclusion. But with bewildering simplicity we see the night end, the dawn come in and a wild thing approach a garden. . . . But the compression without being crowded, the opposite of being squeezed into a narrow space, a few lines, a universe, from the milky way . . . vividly appears before us.

But where has it been hidden? because it is somewhere among the words to our despair, if we are poets, or pretend to be, it is really a simple miracle, like that of the loaves and the fishes . . .

Where does the miracle lodge, to have survived so unaffectedly the years, translation to a foreign language and not only a foreign language but a language of fundamentally different aspect from that in which the words were first written? The metaphor is total, it is overall, a total metaphor.

But there are two parts to every metaphor that we have known heretofore:

the object and its reference—one of them is missing in these Chinese poems that have survived to us and survived through the years, to themselves also. They have been jealously, lovingly guarded. . . . Where does it exist in the fabric of the poem? so tough that it can outlast copper and steel . . . a poem?

—and really laughs and cries! it is alive.
—It is as frightening as it is good.

And the Chinese as a race have built upon it to survive, the words of Tu Fu, a drunken poet, what I mean is DRUNK! and a bum, who did not do perhaps one constructive thing with himself in his life—or a Bodenheim.

I go to a reception and find a room crowded with people whom I cannot talk with except one, a man (or a woman perhaps) or one who wearies me with his insistencies. . . . When a few miraculous lines that keep coming into my head transport me through space a thousand years into the past. . . .

"A magic carpet" the ancients called it. It costs nothing, it's not the least EXPENSIVE!

Look at the object: an unhappy woman, no longer young, waking in her lonely bed and looking over a moonlit valley, that is all. Or a man drunk or playing with his grandchildren who detain him so that he cannot keep an appointment to visit a friend. . . . And what? A few fragile lines which have proved indestructible!

Have you ever thought that a cannon blast or that of an atomic bomb is absolutely powerless beside this?—unless you extinguish man (and woman), the whole human race. A smile would supersede it, totally.

> I raise the curtains and go out
> To watch the moon. Leaning on the
> Balcony, I breathe the evening
> Wind from the west, heavy with the
> Odors of decaying Autumn.
> The rose jade of the river
> Blends with the green jade of the void.
> Hidden in the grass a cricket chirps.
> Hidden in the sky storks cry out.
> I turn over and over in
> My heart the memories of
> Other days. Tonight as always
> There is no one to share my thoughts.
>
> *Chu Shu Chen*

or this:

VISITORS

I have had asthma for a
Long time. It seems to improve
Here in this house by the river.
It is quiet too. No crowds
Bother me. I am brighter here
And more rested. I am happy here.
When someone calls at my thatched hut
My son brings me my straw hat
And I go out to gather
A handful of fresh vegetables.
It isn't much to offer.
But it is given in friendship.

Tu Fu

These men (a woman among the best of them) were looking at direct objects when they were writing, the transition from their pens or brushes is direct to the page. It was a beautiful object (not always a beautiful object, sometimes a horrible one) that they produced. It is incredible that it survived. It must have been treasured as a rare phenomenon by the people to be cared for and reproduced at great pains.

But the original inscriptions, so vividly recording the colors and moods of the scene . . . were invariably put down graphically in the characters (not words), the visual symbols that night and day appeared to the poet. The Chinese calligraphy must have contributed vastly to this.

Our own "Imagists" were right to brush aside purely grammatical conformations. What has grammar to do with poetry save to trip up its feet in that mud? It is important to a translator but that is all. But it is important to a translator, as Kenneth Rexroth well knows. But mostly he has to know the construction of his own idiom into which he is rendering his text, when to ignore its more formal configurations.

This is where the translations that Kenneth Rexroth has made are brilliant. His knowledge of the American idiom has given him complete freedom to make a euphonious rendering of a text which has defied more cultured ears to this date. It may seem to be undisciplined but it is never out of the translator's measured control. Mr. Rexroth is a genius in his own right, inventing a modern language, or following a vocal tradition which he raises here to great distinction. Without a new language into which the poems could be rendered their meaning would have been lost.

TU FU

"Tu Fu is, in my opinion, and in the opinion of a majority of those qualified to speak, the greatest non-epic, non-dramatic poet who has survived in any language."

This is certainly true, but it dodges the issue—what kind of poet is Tu Fu? Not epic, not dramatic, but not in any accepted sense lyric either. Although many of his poems, along with others of the T'ang Dynasty, have been sung from that day to this, and although the insistent rhythms, rhymes, and tonal patterns of Chinese verse are lost in free-verse translation so that we do not realize how musical even the most irregular Chinese verse is (the most irregular, curiously enough, owes its very irregularity to the fact that it was written to pre-existing melodies), almost none of Tu Fu's verse is lyric in the sense in which the songs of Shakespeare, Thomas Campion, Goethe, or Sappho are lyric.

Rather, his is a poetry of reverie, comparable to Leopardi's "L'Infinito," which might well be a translation from the Chinese, or the better sonnets of Wordsworth. This kind of elegiac reverie has become the principal form of modern poetry, as poetry has ceased to be a public art and has become, as Whitehead said of religion, "What man does with his aloneness."

It is this convergence of sensibilities across the barriers of time, space, and culture that accounts for the great popularity of Chinese poetry in translation today, and for its profound influence on all major modern American poets. In addition, Tu Fu, although he was by no means "alienated" and at war with society like Baudelaire, was in fact cut off from it and spent his life, after a brief career as a high official of Ming Huang, The Bright Emperor, as a wandering exile. His poetry is saturated with the exile's nostalgia and the abiding sense of the pathos of glory and power. In addition, he shares with Baudelaire and Sappho, his only competitors in the West, an exceptionally exacerbated sensibility, acute past belief. You feel that Tu Fu brings to each poetic situation, each experienced complex of sensations and values, a completely open nervous system. Out of this comes the choice of imagery—so poignant, so startling, and yet seemingly so ordinary. Later generations of Chinese poets would turn these piercing, uncanny commonplaces into formulas, but in Tu Fu they are entirely fresh, newborn equations of the conscience, and they survive all but the most vulgar translations.

Tu Fu is not faultless. As Court Censor, a kind of Tribune of the Patricians, under Su Tsung, the son of Ming Huang, he seems to have been a cantankerous courtier. He took his sinecure job seriously and, an unregenerate believer in the Confucian classics, proceeded to admonish the Emperor on his morals and foreign policy. He was dismissed and spent the rest of his life wandering over China. He stayed longest in his famous grass hut in the suburbs of Ch'eng Tu in Szechuan. As the dynasty disintegrated and China entered on an interregnum, a time of troubles, he started wandering again, slowly, down the great river, always longing for the capital. His last years were spent on a houseboat, and on it, at 59, he died, possibly from overexposure during a flood and storm.

This is a troubled enough life, but Tu Fu writes of it with a melancholy that often verges on self-pity. He is a valetudinarian. By 30, he was calling himself a white-haired old man. He always speaks of his home as a grass hut and presents himself as being very poor. Actually, though they were thatched, his various houses were probably quite palatial, and he seems never to have relinquished ownership of any of them and always to have drawn revenue from the farms attached to them. He had the mildest literary affection for his wife, whom he did not see for many years. He wrote no love poems to women; as with most of his caste, his passionate relationships were with men. Much of this is just convention, the accepted tone of Chinese poetry of the scholar gentry. Tu Fu's faults are microscopic in comparison with the blemishes that cover Baudelaire like blankets. Behind Baudelaire's carapace is a sensibility always struggling for transcendence. In Tu Fu the vision of spiritual reality is immanent and suffuses every item presented to the senses. Behind the conventions, behind the faults which make him human and kin to all of us, are a wisdom and a humanness as profound as Homer's.

No other great poet is as completely secular as Tu Fu. He comes from a more mature, saner culture than Homer, and it is not even necessary for him to say that the gods, the abstractions from the forces of nature and the passions of men, are frivolous, lewd, vicious, quarrelsome, and cruel and that only the steadfastness of human loyalty, magnanimity, compassion redeem the nightbound world. For Tu Fu, the realm of being and value is not bifurcated. The Good, the True, and the Beautiful are not an Absolute, set over against an inchoate reality that always struggles, unsuccessfully, to approximate the pure value of the absolute. Reality is dense, all one being. Values are the way we see things. This is the essence of the Chinese world view, and it overrides even the most ethereal Buddhist philosophizing and distinguishes it from its Indian sources. There is nothing that is absolutely omnipotent, but there is nothing that is purely contingent either.

Tu Fu is far from being a philosophical poet in the ordinary sense, yet no Chinese poetry embodies more fully the Chinese sense of the unbreakable wholeness of reality. The quality is the quantity; the value is the fact. The metaphor, the symbols are not conclusions drawn from the images; they are the images themselves in concrete relationship. It is this immediacy of utterance that has made Chinese poetry in translation so popular with modern Western poets. The complicated historical and literary references and echoes disappear; the vocal effects cannot be transmitted. What comes through, stripped of all accessories, is the simple glory of the facts—the naked, transfigured poetic situation.

The concept of the poetic situation is itself a major factor in almost all Chinese poems of any period. Chinese poets are not rhetorical; they do not talk about the material of poetry or philosophize abstractly about life—they present a scene and an action. "The north wind tears the banana leaves." It is South China in the autumn. "A lonely goose flies south across the setting sun." Autumn again, and evening. "Smoke rises from the rose jade animal to the painted rafters." A palace. "She toys idly with the strings of an inlaid lute." A concubine. "Suddenly one snaps beneath her jeweled fingers." She is tense and tired of waiting for her master. This is not the subject matter, but it is certainly the method, of almost all the poets of the modern, international idiom, whether Pierre Reverdy or Francis Jammes, Edwin Muir or William Carlos Williams, Quasimodo or the early, and to my taste best, poems of Rilke.

If Isaiah is the greatest of all religious poets, then Tu Fu is irreligious. But to me his is the only religion likely to survive the Time of Troubles that is closing out the twentieth century. It can be understood and appreciated only by the application of what Albert Schweitzer called "reverence for life." What is, is what is holy. I have translated a considerable amount of his poetry, and I have saturated myself with him for forty years. He has made me a better man, a more sensitive perceiving organism, as well as, I hope, a better poet. His poetry answers out of hand the question that worries aestheticians and critics, "What is poetry for?" What his poetry does superlatively is what is the purpose of all art.

HSIEH'S SHOES

The people of mainstream China call themselves *"Han"* people, even today. The term is contrasted with any and all "ethnic" groupings—such as the people of the south known as the *Yüeh* (modern *Viet* of Vietnam), who "cut their hair short and tattooed themselves." (These days, cadres organizing and educating in Tibet who are too grossly contemptuous of local customs might be sent back labeled "Han chauvinists.")

Even in the fourth century A.D. we can assume that the forests and agriculturally marginal areas of greater China were inhabited, even if thinly, by either backwoods Han people or tribal people.

The post-Han "Six Dynasties" period witnessed a flourishing back-to-nature movement from within the ruling gentry class, a "nature" that extended from the fields and gardens of the suburbs to the really deep hills. Many people who might in less turbulent times have exercised their class prerogative of administrative employment turned instead toward an idea of purity and simplicity. Not all were wealthy or self-indulgent. The poet Tao Yuan-ming (Tao Ch'ien) (365–427) was a minor official whose early retirement to a small farm was his own choice. His poems are still the standard of a certain quietness, openness, emptiness, and also human frankness and frailty in the confusions of farm, family, and wine, that much later Chinese poetry aspires to. The Taoist idea of being nobody in the world, "behind instead of in front," gave strength to those who often must have missed the social life of their urban *literati* friends as they sat up late reading and drinking alone in their estates or homesteads out amongst the peasants.

Some of the Han Dynasty poems portray the wild mountain world as horrible and scary. As Burton Watson points out, a gradual shift in the mode of *seeing* nature took place. In the songs of the *Classic of Songs*, which reflect so much of the life of the people, plants were named specifically; the scene was the ground and brush right before one—where one danced or harvested. By the Six Dynasties, the view moved back and became more panoramic. A case in point is the work of the poet Hsieh Ling-yün (385–433)—who has only a few rare poetic ancestors in earlier China. His aristocratic family had moved south, and he grew up in a biome that would have been considered exotic and barbarous by Confucius.

Hsieh was a lover of mountains. His fascination with the densely wooded, steep hills of South China (peaking between 4,000 and 6,000 feet) took him on long climbs and rambles, including one month-long trail-cutting exploration. He combined in himself would-be Taoist recluse and vigorous wilderness adventurer. An early follower of Buddhism (a new thing at that time, limited to upper-class circles), he wrote an essay expounding "instant enlightenment."

Hsieh's ambivalent pursuit of success in politics ended when he was banished to a minor position in a remote south coast town; he soon resigned totally from the administration and moved to a run-down family estate in the hills southeast of present-day Hangchow. The place and life there is detailed in his long *fu* ("prose poem") called *Living in the Mountains*. The farther and nearer landscapes are described in detail. The fish, birds, plants, and mammals are listed. The whole is seen as an ideal place for pursuing Taoist and Buddhist meditations. Thus,

> I cast no lines for fish.
> I spread no nets for hare.
> I have no use for barbed shafts.
> Who would set out rabbit snares or fish traps?

And he says he "awoke to the complete propriety of loving what lives." Later in the poetical essay he describes his workers, "felling trees; they clear the thorns and cut bamboo," and sundry bark and reed and rush gathering activities; and charcoal-making. This faint contradiction, intensified later in history, can become a major problem: individual animals' lives are carefully spared, while the habitat that sustains them is heedlessly destroyed.

Hsieh is a puzzle. Arrogant and overbearing at court, he made enemies there. Intensely intellectual as a Buddhist, and careless of the needs or feelings of local people, he managed to get intrigued into a charge of rebellion, and was beheaded in the marketplace. Hsieh was probably already out of place in China—he should have joined the Rock Mountain Fur Company and gone out to be a trapper. He was "wild," and as an aristocrat that took some contradictory and nasty turns. But he opened up the landscape—"mountains and waters"—to the poetic consciousness for all time, and he was a fine poet.

Mountains were always foci of spirit power in China, beginning perhaps as habitat for the *hsien*, a shaman who gained "power" in the hills. Later they became a place of retreat for the Taoist practitioner of "harmonizing with the Way" and again as sites for Buddhist monasteries. Hsieh Ling-yün plunged into the watercourses and thickets, camped in the heights alone, walked all night in the moonlight. These years and energies lie behind what we now take to be the Chinese sense of nature as reflected in art. Hsieh is also remembered as the inventor of a unique mountaineering shoe or clog—no one is quite sure how it looked.

EMPTY MOUNTAIN

China is wide. Travel was mostly on foot, maybe with a packhorse, sometimes also a riding horse. In the lowlands a network of canals provided channels for slow-moving passenger boats as well as freight barges. Travelers moved by boat on the big rivers, slowly and laboriously upstream, pulled by men on shore, and swiftly and boisterously back down. Boats sailed across the lakes and slow-moving lower river reaches. Horse and ox carts moved men and materials in the alluvial plains and rolling hills. In the mountains and deserts, long caravans of pack animals moved the goods of empire.

Government officials were accustomed to traveling weeks or even months to a new appointment, with their whole family. Buddhist monks and Taoist wanderers had a tradition of freely walking for months or years on end. In times of turmoil whole populations of provinces, and contending armies, might be tangled in frenzied travel on the paths and waterways. It was said, "If a man has his heart set on great things 10,000 *li* are his front yard." So the people of the watersheds of the Yang and Huang rivers came to know the shape of their territory.

The officials and monks (and most poets were one or the other) were an especially mobile group of literate people. Travelers' prose or rhymed-prose descriptions of landscapes were ingenious in evoking the complexity of gorges and mountains. Regional geographies with detailed accounts of local biomes were encouraged. Hsieh Ling-yün's *fu* on his mountain place is descriptive and didactic—but his poems in the *shih* (lyric) form already manifest the quiet intensity that becomes the definitive quality of Chinese *shih* poetry in its greatest creative T'ang and Sung Dynasty phases.

The Chinese and Japanese traditions carry within them the most sensitive, mind-deepening poetry of the natural world ever written by civilized people. Because these poets were men and women who dealt with budgets, taxes, penal systems, and the overthrow of governments, they had a heart-wrenching grasp of the contradictions that confront those who love the natural world and are yet tied to the civilized. This must be one reason why Chinese poetry is so widely appreciated by contemporary Occidentals.

Yet it's hard to pin down what a "Chinese nature poem" might be, and why it is so effective. They are not really about landscapes or scenery. Space of distant hills becomes space in life; a condition the poet-critic Lu Chi called "calm transparency." Mountains and rivers were seen to be the visible expression of cosmic principles; the cosmic principles go back into silence, non-being, emptiness; a Nothing that can produce the ten thousand things, and the ten thousand things will have that marvelous emptiness still at the center. So the poems are also "silent." Much is left unsaid, and the reverberation or mirroring—a flight of birds across the mind of the sky—leaves an afterimage to be savored, and finally leaves no trace. The Chinese poetic tradition is also where human emotions are revealed; where a still official can be vulnerable and frail. Lu Chi says poetry starts with a lament for fleeting life, and regard for the myriad growing things—taking thought of the great virtuous deeds of people past, and the necessity of making "maps" for the future. Chinese poetry steps out of narrow human-centered affairs into a big-spirited world of long time, long views, and natural processes; and comes back to a brief moment in a small house by a fence.

The strain of nostalgia for the self-contained hard-working but satisfying life of the farmer goes along somehow with delight in jumbled gorges. Nature is finally not a "wilderness" but a habitat, the best of habitats, a place where you not only practice meditation or strive for a vision, but grow vegetables, play games with the children, and drink wine with friends. In this there is a politics of a special order—the Chinese nature poet is harking back to the Neolithic village, never forgotten and constantly returned to mind by the Taoist classics—as a model for a better way of life. Sectarian Taoism and its secret societies fermented a number of armed peasant uprisings through history that unwittingly had "Neolithic" on their standards. "Playing with your grandchildren"—"growing chrysanthemums"—"watching the white clouds"—are phrases from a dream of pre-feudal or post-revolutionary society.

Chinese poets of these centuries were not biologists or primitive hunters, though, and their poetics did not lead them to certain precisions. What they found were landscapes to match inner moods—and a deep sense of reverence for this mystery of a real world. In Burton Watson's analysis of nature imagery in T'ang poems he finds more references to non-living phenomena than living, and more than half of those looking upward to sky, weather, wind, clouds, and moon. Downward, rivers, waters, and mountains predominate. Among living things willow and pine are the most-mentioned trees, but the specific names of herbaceous plants and flowers are few—with "flowers" usually meaning the blossoms of trees like cherry or peach. Wild goose is the most common bird, associated with being separated from a friend; and monkey the most common mammal—because of its mournful cry. Cicada and moth are the most common insects. Many natural references, then, are used for their symbolic or customary human associations, and not for intrinsic natural qualities. No doubt the oral poetry of a pre-literate people will have more acquaintance with the actual living creatures as numinous intelligences in furry or scaly bodies. But this does not detract from what the Chinese poems are, highly disciplined and formal poems that open us to the dilemma of having "regard for the myriad growing things" while being literate monks or administrators or wives of officials in the world's first "great society." The reign of the Emperor Hsuan Tsung (712–756) is considered one of the high points of Chinese cultural history: the poets Wang Wei, Li Po, and Tu Fu were at the height of their powers during those years, and so were the brilliant and influential Ch'an Masters Shen-hui, Nan-yüeh, Ma-tsu, and Po-chang. The national population may have been as high as 60 million.

I first came onto Chinese poems in translation at 19, when my ideal of nature was a 45-degree ice slope on a volcano, or an absolutely virgin rain forest. They helped me to "see" fields, farms, tangles of brush, the azaleas in the back of an old brick apartment. They freed me from excessive attachment to wild mountains, with their way of suggesting that even the wildest hills are places where people, also, live.

> Empty mountains:
>   no one to be seen,
> Yet—hear—
>   human sounds and echoes.
> Returning sunlight
>   enters the dark woods;
> Again shining
>   on green moss, above.
> *Wang Wei*

DISTANT HILLS

For those men who passed the civil service examinations and accepted official posts, travel from place to place became a way of life. They were commonly transferred every three years. Su Shih was born in Szechwan near the foot of Mount Omei in 1037. Like many who rose to political and literary eminence in the Sung, he came from relatively humble people, "connected with the local weaving industry." His grandfather had been illiterate. He and his younger brother were locally tutored by a Taoist priest. Together with their father they traveled the thousand-mile journey down the Yangtze and north to the capital of K'ai-feng, where both boys passed the examinations the first try, a striking feat. In his early poem "On the Yangtze Watching the Hills" (traveling by boat with his father and brother through the San-hsia Gorge) Su Shih opens some of that space for us:

> From the boat watching hills—swift horses:
> a hundred herds race by in a flash.
> Ragged peaks before us suddenly change shape,
> Ranges behind us start and rush away.
> I look up: a narrow trail angles back and forth,
> A man walking it, high in the distance.
> I wave from the deck, trying to call,
> But the sail takes us south like a soaring bird.[1]

All three were given employment. In 1066 the father died and the two sons returned to bury him in Szechwan. It was the last time Su Shih saw his native village. He was 29.

This mobility contributes to the impression we get from Su and his cohorts that they no longer cared about particular landscapes. Indeed, for many of them there was no place in China they called home enough to know the smells and the wild plants, but during their interminable journeys on river boats and canal barges the scenery slowly unrolled for them like a great scroll. At the same time there was a cheerful recognition and acceptance of the fact that "we live in society." The clear, dry, funny poems of daily life with family and neighbors that came of this are marvelous. Taoist ideas of living in mountain isolation, or breaking conventions, came to be seen as romantic and irresponsible. Yoshikawa comments on the optimism of Sung poetry, and suggests that it echoes the optimism of the ancient *Classic of Songs (Shih Ching)*, with its

---

1 Su Tung-P'o, *Selections from a Sung Dynasty Poet*, Burton Watson, tr. (New York: Columbia University Press, 1965) p. 23.

care for daily tasks and the busy space within the farmyard. The dominant emotion expressed in T'ang dynasty writing is sorrow and grief: humankind is all too impermanent, only mountains and rivers will remain.[2] Sung poets like Mei Yao-ch'en might write in rough plain language, or a low-key style, of things the elegantly intense T'ang poets would never touch. Such is Yang Wan-li's poem on a fly:

> Noted outside the window: a fly, the sun on his back,
> rubbing his legs together, relishing the morning brightness.
> Sun and shadow about to shift—already he knows it,
> Suddenly flies off, to hum by a different window.[3]

Su Shih, lying on his back in a boat, takes detachment a step further:

> I greet the breeze that happens along
> And lift a cup to offer to the vastness:
> How pleasant—that we have no thought of each other![4]

Kojiro Yoshikawa's brief analysis of nature images in Sung poetry notes that "sunset" is a common reference in the T'ang with a strong overtone of sadness. Su Shih, writing on a sunset seen from a Buddhist temple:

> Faint wind: on the broad water,
>   wrinkles like creases in a shoe:
> Broken clouds: over half the sky,
>   a red the color of fish tails.[5]

Rain, Yoshikawa observes, is a frequent Sung reference—rain to listen to at night while talking with a bedmate, rain to burn incense and study by.

> Shall I tell you the way to become a god
>   in this humdrum world?
> Burn some incense and sit listening to the rain.
>
> *Lu Yu*[6]

2   Kojiro Yoshikawa, *An Introduction to Sung Poetry*, Burton Watson, tr. (Cambridge: Harvard University Press, 1967), p. 25.

3   Burton Watson, *Chinese Lyricism* (New York: Columbia University Press, 1971), p. 202.

4   Yoshikawa, p. 23.

5   Yoshikawa, p. 47.

6   Yoshikawa, p. 48.

In a society of such mobility, complexity, and size, it is to be expected that a "sense of place" would be hard to maintain. Humanistic concerns can be cultivated anywhere, but certain kinds of understanding and information about the natural world are only available to those who stay put and keep looking. There is another kind of "staying put" that flourished in some circles during the Sung, namely the meditation practice of Ch'an Buddhism, zazen. What some Sung poets and thinkers might have lost in sense of natural place was balanced to some extent by a better understanding of natural self. A different sort of grounding occurred.

Much of the distinctive quality of Sung poetry can be attributed to the influence of the relentless and original Su Shih. Su was also an advanced Ch'an practicer, which is evident in his resolute, penetrating, sensitive body of work. The Ch'an influence is not at its best in the poems about monks or temples; we find it in plainer places. But when Su says of the sky, "How pleasant—that we have no thought of each other" it should not be taken as an expression of the heartlessness or remoteness of nature. Within the mutual mindlessness of sky and self the Ch'an practicer enacts the vivid energy and form of each blade of grass, each pebble. The obsession that T'ang poets had with impermanence was a sentimental response to the commonly perceived stress of Mahayana Buddhism on transience and evanescence. Ch'an teachers never bothered with self-pity. They brought a playful and courageous style of give-and-take to the study of impermanent phenomena. I suspect that Sung poets were more dyed with the true spirit of Ch'an than those of the T'ang. From the standpoint of the natural environment, the T'ang view can almost be reversed—it seems the mountains and rivers, or at least their forests and creatures, soils and beds, are more fragile than we thought. Human beings grimly endure.

CHINESE POETRY AND THE AMERICAN IMAGINATION
[STATEMENTS FROM A SYMPOSIUM, APRIL 1977]

Kenneth Rexroth:

Chinese poetry began to influence writers in English with the translations into French of Hervey St. Denis and others in the mid-19th century who translated *Three Hundred Poems of the T'ang* into French free verse. If American and English poets did not read French, the translations of Herbert Giles and other Sinologists like him were practically worthless, because of the doggerel verse in which they were rendered. Probably the most influential was Judith Gautier's *Le livre de Jade*, which was translated by E. Powys Mathers in *Colored Stars* and *A Garden of Bright Waters*. Neither Gautier nor Mathers read Chinese and, in fact, her informant was a Thai who didn't read Chinese either. Nevertheless, these prose poems (which first appeared in Stuart Merrill's *Pastels in Prose)* came across as deeply moving poetry in English.

Approximately contemporarily appeared the first translations by Arthur Waley and, not long after, Ezra Pound's *Cathay*. Pound and Waley taught the West a kind of irregular iambic pentameter or free verse, in both cases as dependent on quantitative rhythms as on accentual. Chinese poetry, in fact, bears no resemblance to this kind of verse. It is rhymed with considerable emphasis, usually, on the rhymed words, and at first was in four monosyllable lines, or five, or seven, and in addition the tones which distinguished the meanings of homonymous Chinese monosyllables came to follow regular patterns. Later in the T'ang, and reaching its flower in the Sung Dynasty, poems were patterned on the irregular lines of songs, as well as being written in the five or seven syllable classic patterns.

Learned and industrious people have tried to reproduce in English the original rhythms, but have managed to produce only absurdities. So Chinese poetry has come to influence the West as a special form of Chinese verse— which annoys some more pedantic Sinologists of Chinese ancestry. It is a special kind of free verse and its appearance happened to converge with the movement toward Objectivism, Imagism, and even the Cubist poetry of Gertrude Stein and Pierre Reverdy—"no ideas but in things," as Williams says rather naively.

There is almost no rhetorical verse of the kind we find in Augustan Latin and later in Renaissance poetry throughout Europe, nor is there the luxuriously foliate poetry of India (with the possible exception of the *Li Sao*). There are no true poetic epics in Chinese poetry. The heroic epic of China is an historical novel, *The Romance of Three Kingdoms*. And, until recent years, the verse of Chinese drama was considered beneath serious literary consideration, although, for instance, "The Flower Burying Song" from the play taken from *The Dream of the Red Chamber* is quite impressive poetry. There are verse treatises in Chinese comparable to Virgil's *Georgics* or Horace's *Art of Poetry*, but even they follow the tendency toward direct presentation of concrete images.

Most Chinese poetry, whether elegiac or love poetry, situates the reader in a definite *mise-en-scène*. "The driving wind and rain tear the banana leaves"— we are in the South. "The swallows huddle in their nest under the gilded rafters"—a palace. "I am too weary to pick up my jade inlaid lute"—probably a concubine. "Soon the wild geese will be returning from the North, but they will bring me no message"—he is away fighting the Northern Barbarians. This can become a facile formula, especially when, in the later dynasties, the lines were arranged in strictly parallel couplets, but it is certainly a way to produce effective—affective—poetry, if you are a poet. In fact, it differs little from the poetry envisaged by Wordsworth and Coleridge in the preface to *Lyrical Ballads* and often realized in their best poems. But so true is it also of Horace's "Under Soracte" or the best poems of Hafiz or the rare poignant imagistic moments in Tennyson's "In Memoriam."

Chinese poetry entered the American and, to a much lesser degree, English poetic consciousness at exactly the right moment to purge the rhetoric and moralizing of 19th century Romantic poetry and the even more moralistic, preachy poetry of the '90s. Much of the poetry of Ernest Dowson is little sermons of disappointed Epicureanism.

Japanese poetry, which after all is an extremely compressed expression of Chinese aesthetics, became popular among American poets at about the same time and through the same people—Pound, Waley, and Mathers. Today, for a very large sector of American poets, the poetry of the Far East is more influential than 19th and 20th century French poetry, which has dominated the international idiom for so long, and certainly incomparably more influential than American or English poetry of the 19th century. The only rival is the slowly dying influence of "metaphysical" verse of the English Renaissance. It would be possible to name over a hundred American poets deeply influenced by the poetry of the Far East and some who have difficulty in thinking about poetry in any other idiom than Chinese or Japanese. Now, of course, there are a number of poets, by no means uninfluential, who read Chinese and Japanese and who are philosophically Buddhist or Taoist or both.

Gary Snyder:

The fact is that although first and foremost the translations of Ezra Pound, Arthur Waley, a little later Witter Bynner, have had a distinctive impact on people's thinking and people's poetics, there was another thing that has been very important, running parallel to that right through, and that has been the idea of the Chinese poet, the image that the Chinese poet as a poet, as role-model, presented to us.

In a simple way, I think, our first Anglo-American received view of the Chinese poets was that they were civil servants. And in a simplified way, there is some truth in this. There were extremes as great perhaps as Han Yu on the one side as a rigorous, benevolent, socially-minded poet, Confucianist all his life; and at the other end, perhaps a poet like Han Shan, who speaks entirely from the hermit's habitat. Yet in actual fact, these two kinds of poetry, which I am artificially separating for the moment, were generally produced by the same people. Now to add to the complexity, we have no real models in Occidental poetry of poets who either were staunch, quiet, solid civil servants involved in responsible positions in society for a whole lifetime as a regular type of poet, nor do we have on the other hand a real tradition of hermit's poetry in the Occident. So it's all the more interesting to see that these two types of roles of poetry were both in China coming from the same individuals, often at different stages within one lifetime, or in some cases, it was just a matter of literally changing hats—Confucian hat to Taoist hat while on a trip to the country.

I first responded, in 1949, living in Oregon, to my contact with Chinese poetry on the level of nature; that was what I was interested in. As a student of anthropology beginning to read on Far Eastern matters but really focusing on American Indian studies, I was deeply concerned with the almost abstract questions of philosophy of nature and problems involved when high civilizations impact on nature and impact on natural peoples. As a mountaineer and back-packer, when I read Chinese poetry, I was struck in some of the translations by qualities hard to describe . . . clarity, limpidity, space, and at the same time, a fine, specialized and precise attention and observation of natural detail—natural detail existing and functioning within a very large, 10,000 *li*, moonlit territory. That was my first interest in it.

Later, of course, reading more widely, and still only in translations, I realized that the extent was quite a bit broader, that it went from the *Shih Ching* (known variously as *The Book of Odes*, *The Book of Songs*, and *The Confucian Odes*) to, say, Ming Dynasty (1368–1644), *Shih Ching* to Mao Tse-tung, and that it included a vast range of possibilities of content. I also see now how different American poets came to Chinese poetry and received different things. As I looked initially only to the hermit poet/nature poet for inspiration and for a while took that to be what Chinese poetry really was, so a man whose work I valued highly as a teacher in poetic technology, namely Ezra Pound, found in Chinese poetry something else entirely. Pound was delighted with the possibility of poets having political power in a strong bureaucracy. Those perhaps are the two extremes—myself or someone like myself, and Pound or someone like Pound—in their reactions to the role possibilities implied in Chinese poetry.

Then we begin to notice something else there, lurking slightly below the surface, slightly further back in time—we see a glimmering in Li Ho, it's there very clearly in the *Ch'-u T'zu (The Songs of the South)*, and we can discern it in certain features in the *Shih Ching*—and that is the poet as shaman. The shaman-poet role has been explicated for us by Edward Schafer's recent work, *The Divine Woman*, that brings out a whole range of images and symbols and underlying energies that are in that poetry, that you might not see there at first glance.

And yet, to go one more step, finally, for myself, what I go back to Chinese poetry for is its humaneness. I'm going to go back for a second to the introduction to the *Shih Ching* (compiled *circa* 600 B.C.), the original classic collection/anthology. "Poetry is to regulate the married couple, establish the principle of filial piety, intensify human relationships, elevate civilization, and improve public morals." That's Confucius' estimate, or somebody like Confucius, of what poetry should do; and it must have had great influence because that man was highly respected in later centuries. Thinking this one through again, I thought: well, there's a lot of truth in what he says, and actually poetry in a healthy, stable society (in which poets are not forced willy-nilly to all be alienated revolutionaries) does influence the behavior of lovers, and it does make one think of one's parents, and put importance on friendship, and give meaning to history and culture, and improve public manners. So then I thought, yes, poetry should do that. Actually, in a visionary way, what we want poetry to do is guide lovers toward ecstasy, give witness to the dignity of old people, intensify human bonds, elevate the community, and improve public spirit. And so, it is in just that humaneness, that delicate—I'm almost tempted to use the word sweet—appreciation of the details of human life, families, the frustrations of employment with the government, and the frustrations of being a hermit, that we perhaps respond to most deeply in Chinese poetry, having a poetry ourselves which is so different in a way, so mythological, so political and so elevated, that it can't deal with ordinary human affairs often.

ON PO CHÜ-I

In *The Analects*, Confucius says: "There are three hundred songs in *The Book of Songs*, but this one phrase tells it all: *thoughts never twisty*" (II.2). *The Book of Songs* is the ancient source from which the Chinese poetic tradition flows, and *thoughts never twisty* may very well describe the essence of the entire tradition as well, for it is a tradition that consistently valued clarity and depth of wisdom, not mere complexity and virtuosity. In this, Po Chü-i (772–846 C.E.) is the quintessential Chinese poet, for although it deeply informs the work of all the major ancient poets, Po makes that sage clarity itself his particular vision.

Po Chü-i was a more serious student of Ch'an (Zen) Buddhism than any mainstream poet up to his time, and it was Ch'an that gave much of the clarity and depth to his life and work. Po's poems often include the explicit use of Ch'an ideas, indeed he is the poet who really opened mainstream poetry to Buddhist experience, his work becoming a major source of information on Buddhist practice in his time. But it is in the poetics shaping Po's poetry that Ch'an is more fundamentally felt. In Ch'an practice, the self and its constructions of the world are dissolved away until nothing remains but empty mind or "no-mind." This empty mind is often spoken of as mirroring the world, leaving its ten thousand things utterly simple, utterly themselves, and utterly sufficient. That suggests one possible Ch'an poetry: an egoless poetry which renders the ten thousand things in such a way that they empty the self as they shimmer with the clarity of their own self-sufficient identity. Po wrote a number of poems in this mode, but the great master of this poetics was Wang Wei (701–761), whose brief poems resound with the selfless clarity of no-mind:

DEER PARK

No one seen. In empty mountains,
a hint of drifting voice, no more.

Entering these deep woods, late sun-
light ablaze on green moss, rising.

The other possible Ch'an poetry is that of an egoless ego. Empty mind would seem to preclude the possibility of a personal poetry such as Po's. The quiet response of even the most reticent poem is still a construction, as Po knew well: he playfully says numerous times that his Ch'an practice has failed because he could not overcome his "poetry demon," his "word-karma." Po's response to experience seems to have been quite passionate—whether the experience was as monumental as poverty and war, or as ordinary as tea and an afternoon nap—and this full heart was of course the engine driving his prolific output as a poet. Po had hoped that Ch'an practice might quell his passionate responses, and this certainly did happen to some extent, but it seems he came to realize that the self is also one of those ten thousand things that are utterly themselves and sufficient. Taoist thought would describe this insight rather differently, as the realization that self is always already selfless, for it is but a momentary form among the constant transformation of earth's ten thousand things. This is a crucial conjunction of Ch'an and Taoist philosophy, and no doubt a major reason Po considered them to be two aspects of the same system. In any case, this insight results in a poetry quite different from Wang Wei's. Rather than Wang Wei's strategy of losing the self among the ten thousand things, this poetics opens the poem to the various movements of self, and Po Chü-i was a master of its subtle ways. In a culture that made no fundamental distinction between heart and mind, he inhabited everyday experience at the level where a simple heart is a full heart and a simple mind is an empty mind, endowing *thoughts never twisty* with new depths. Such is his gentle power: the sense in his poems of dwelling at the very center of one's life, combining the intimacies of a full heart and the distances of an empty mind.

Po found his full heart and empty mind most completely realized in the practice of idleness. This idleness is also central to the work of T'ao Ch'ien (365–427), the poet who originated the poetic world which defines the Chinese tradition. Etymologically, the character for idleness which T'ao Ch'ien used (*hsien*) connotes "profound serenity and quietness," its pictographic elements rendering a tree standing alone within the gates to a courtyard, or in its alternate form, moonlight shining through an open door. Po Chü-i often uses this character as well, but he also uses another character: *lan*. The pictographic elements of this character are equally revealing: it is made up of the character for "trust" (*lai*) beside the character for "heart-mind" (*hsin*). Hence, the heart-mind of trust, the heart-mind of trust in the world. But this is trust of truly profound dimensions, for "idleness" is essentially a lazybones word for a spiritual posture known as *wu-wei*. *Wu-wei* is a central concept in Taoism, where it is associated with *tzu-jan*, the mechanism of Tao's process. *Tzu-jan*'s literal meaning is "self-so" or "the of-itself" or "being such of itself," hence "spontaneous" or "natural." But a more descriptive translation might be "occurrence appearing of itself," for it is meant to describe the ten thousand things unfolding spontaneously, each according to its own nature. For Taoists, we dwell as an organic part of *tzu-jan* by practicing *wu-wei*, which literally means "nothing doing," or more descriptively, "selfless action": acting spontaneously as a selfless part of *tzu-jan*, rather than with self-conscious intention. Hence, idleness is a kind of meditative reveling in *tzu-jan*, a state in which daily life becomes the essence of spiritual practice.

Like T'ao Ch'ien's, Po Chü-i's idleness often takes the form of drinking. Drunkenness for Po means, as it generally does in Chinese poetry, drinking just enough wine to achieve a serene clarity of attention, a state in which the isolation of a mind imposing distinctions on the world gives way to a sense of identity with the world. And so again, idleness as a kind of spiritual practice: an utter simplicity of dwelling in which empty mind allows a full heart to move with open clarity. Indeed, Po Chü-i half-seriously spoke of wine rivaling Ch'an as a spiritual practice.

Given his devotion to idleness and the poetics of idleness, Po tends to avoid the kind of imagistic compression more typical of Chinese poetry. For him, the poem is generally a kind of relaxed rambling, open to all thought and experience, whether petty or profound. And not surprisingly, poems are written in exceptionally clear and plain language. Indeed, there is a story that Po always showed his poems to an uneducated old servant-woman, and anything she couldn't understand he rewrote. This poetics also allowed Po to write easily: he wrote a very large number of poems (2,800 survive, far more than any poet before him), and the vast majority of them appear plain and unaccomplished, no different from the work of countless other poets. His poetics suggest that for him such poems would be the most authentically accomplished, for it no doubt reverses the normal criterion for poetry, making poems that are simple and unaccomplished valued above those that push to extremes in shaping experience. But Po doesn't resist the insight that makes striking poems. Surprising insight comes to some of his poems and not to others, and it makes sense that Po doesn't choose among them. So there is a body of poems which walk the fine line where a poem is effortlessly plain and yet surprising and insightful, revealing the profound dimensions of Po's trust in the simple and immediate.

Po Chü-i wrote during the T'ang Dynasty, the period during which Chinese poetry experienced its first great flowering. This renaissance began during the High T'ang period (712–760) in the work of such poets as Wang Wei, Li Po, and Tu Fu, and continued through the Mid-T'ang period (766–835) during which Po Chü-i wrote. Though it hardly ignores life's hardships, the Chinese tradition is grounded in a poetry of balanced affirmation, its great poets speaking primarily of their immediate experience in a natural voice.

But while Po Chü-i was cultivating his pellucid sensibility into the quintessence of this mainstream tradition, a group of poets was experimenting with an alternative poetics which became the most distinctive development during the Mid-T'ang—a poetics of startling disorientations and dream-like hermeticism. This alternative tradition began in the dark extremities of Tu Fu's later work. This work extended the mainstream tradition to its limit, and the stark introspective depths of Meng Chiao's late work (807–814) mark a clear break. Indeed, Meng Chiao's quasi-surreal and symbolist techniques anticipated landmark developments in the modern Western tradition by a millennium, and it is interesting to reconsider the modern avant-garde in light of the alternative Mid-T'ang movement. After Meng Chiao, this movement included a number of major poets and at least two great ones: Li Ho and Li Shang-yin. But its vitality proved rather short-lived, ending with Li Shang-yin's death in 858, though its preoccupations remained dominant for another century, through the feeble Late-T'ang period (836–907), and the reverence accorded its major poets didn't begin to wane for another two centuries. The alternative tradition of Meng Chiao and his heirs made the Mid-T'ang (766–835) an especially rich poetic period, rivaling even its predecessor, the illustrious High T'ang. But Po Chü-i's unassuming poetics proved more enduring than the experimental alternative, for although such poetics result in a modest poetry, it reflects a deep wisdom that was always more admired in China than mere virtuosity and innovation. It was largely through the work of Po Chü-i and other more "conventional" Mid-T'ang poets that the tradition's mainstream was passed on to the next great period of Chinese poetry: the Sung Dynasty, a period in which Ch'an's widespread influence led to a poetry that continued to deepen and expand the possibilities of *thoughts never twisty*.

SOURCES

WILLIAM CARLOS WILLIAMS

Poetry translations from "The Cassia Tree," first published in *New Directions 19* (1966); reprinted in Christopher MacGowan, ed., *The Collected Poems of William Carlos Williams, Vol. II: 1939–1962* (New Directions, 1988). Poems translated 1957–1961 with David Rafael Wang.

"On Rexroth's *One Hundred Poems from the Chinese*": excerpted from "Two New Books by Kenneth Rexroth" [the other is *In Defense of the Earth*] published in *Poetry* (June 1957); reprinted in James E. B. Breslin, ed., *Something to Say: William Carlos Williams on Younger Poets* (New Directions, 1985).

EZRA POUND

Cathay (1915); reprinted and expanded in EP, *Lustra* (1916); reprinted in EP, *Personae* (1926; reprinted by New Directions in 1949); reprinted in EP, *Translations* (New Directions, 1953). The texts here follow the Lea Baechler and A. Walton Litz edition of *Personae* (New Directions, 1990).

The Classic Anthology Defined by Confucius (Harvard Univ. Pr., 1954); reprinted as *The Confucian Odes* by New Directions (1959); reprinted under the original title by Harvard Univ. Pr. (1976).

Ernest Fenollosa & Ezra Pound, *The Chinese Written Character as a Medium for Poetry*; first serialized in *The Little Review* (1919); reprinted in EP, *Instigations* (1920); expanded and reprinted as a separate edition (1936); reprinted by City Lights (1964).

Ch'ü Yüan, Liu Ch'e, and Pan Chieh-yü poems originally published in EP's anthology, *Des Imagistes* (1914). Reprinted in EP, *Lustra* (1916); reprinted in EP, *Personae* (1926). See note to *Cathay* above.

Li Po: "Wine" and Wang Wei: "Dawn on the Mountain," published in *The Little Review* (November 1918) and never collected, other than in facsimile editions.

Li Po: "Calm Night Thought," "The red sun comes out of the Eastern corner," and "Song for the Falling Kingdom"; Wang Wei: "Poor dwelling" and "Sitting in mystic bamboo grove" are drafts of unfinished translations based on the Fenollosa notebooks. The Li Po poems were published in Anne S. Chapple, "Ezra Pound's *Cathay*: Compilation from the Fenollosa Notebooks" (*Paideuma*, Vol. 17, Nos. 2 & 3, Fall & Winter 1988). The Wang Wei poems were published in Zhaoming Qian, *Orientalism and Modernism: The Legacy of China in Pound and Williams* (Duke Univ. Pr., 1995). They have never been collected.

Po Chü-i: "Yin-yo laps in the reeds," undoubtedly based on the Fenollosa manuscripts, was embedded in the second of the "Three Cantos" (the so-called "Ur Cantos," which were radically rewritten as Cantos I–III), published in *Poetry* in June–August 1917. They are now reprinted as an appendix to the Baechler-Litz edition of *Personae* (see above). Previously unidentified as a translation of Po Chü-i.

Anonymous (Han): "She weaves" and "By the river of stars," also from the Fenollosa manuscripts, but written in the late 1950s. Published in Hugh Kenner, *The Pound*

Era (Univ. of California, 1971); "By the river," reprinted in a slightly different version in EP, *Catai*, trans. Mary de Rachewiltz (Milan: Scheiwiller, 1987). Previously unidentified, and never collected.

"Chinese Poetry": published in *To-day* (April 1918) and never collected, other than in facsimile editions.

KENNETH REXROTH

One Hundred Poems from the Chinese (New Directions, 1956).

Love and the Turning Year: One Hundred More Poems from the Chinese (New Directions, 1970).

The Orchid Boat: Women Poets of China (McGraw-Hill, 1972); reprinted as *Women Poets of China* by New Directions (1982). Edited and translated with Ling Chung.

New Poems (New Directions, 1974).

Li Ch'ing Chao: Complete Poems (New Directions, 1979). Edited and translated with Ling Chung.

Liu Tsung-yüan: "A thousand mountains without a bird," from a set of three "Chinese Poems" first published in KR, *The Collected Shorter Poems* (New Directions, 1966).

"Tu Fu": written for KR's "Classics Revisited" column in the *Saturday Review*, (1966); published in book form in KR, *Classics Revisited* (Quadrangle, 1968); reprinted by New Directions (1986).

"Chinese Poetry and the American Imagination": a conference held in New York City in April 1977. The text here is from an untitled photocopied manuscript that was distributed to participants. Partially published in *Ironwood*, No. 17 (1981).

"Poetic Landscape": review of Chang Yin-han & Lewis Walmsley, *Poems by Wang Wei*; published in *The New York Times Book Review*, Dec. 7, 1958; never collected.

GARY SNYDER

Han-shan: first published in *Evergreen Review* (1958); reprinted in book form in GS, *Riprap and Cold Mountain Poems* (Four Seasons Foundation, 1969; reprinted by North Point Press, 1990).

All other translations from *The Gary Snyder Reader* (Counterpoint, 1999).

"Hsieh's Shoes," "Empty Mountain," and "Distant Hills": from an unfinished cultural-ecological history of China, *The Great Clod*, published in *The Gary Snyder Reader*.

"Chinese Poetry and the American Imagination": See Rexroth, above. Published in *Ironwood*, No. 17 (1981).

DAVID HINTON

The Selected Poems of Tu Fu (New Directions, 1989).

The Selected Poems of T'ao Ch'ien (Copper Canyon, 1993).

The Selected Poems of Li Po (New Directions, 1996).

The Late Poems of Meng Chiao (Princeton Univ. Pr., 1996).

The Selected Poems of Po Chü-i (New Directions, 1999).

The Mountain Poems of Hsieh Ling-yün (New Directions, 2001).

Mountain Home: The Wilderness Poetry of Ancient China (Counterpoint, 2002).

"On Po Chü-i": excerpted from the introduction to the *Selected Poems of Po Chü-i*.

ACHILLES FANG

"Lu Ki's 'Rhymeprose on Literature'": revised version published in *New Mexico Quarterly*, Vol. XXII, No. 3 (Autumn, 1952); never collected.

Introduction to *The Confucian Odes*. See Pound, above.

NOTES

Individual poets and collections:

Ch'u Yüan: *Chu Tz'u: The Songs of the South*, trans. David Hawkes (Oxford Univ. Pr., 1959).

Hsieh Ling-yün: J.D. Frodsham, *The Murmuring Stream* (Univ. of Malaya Press, 1967).

Lu Yu: *The Old Man Who Does as He Pleases*, trans. Burton Watson (Columbia Univ. Pr., 1973).

Mei Yao-ch'en: Jonathan Chaves, *Mei Yao-ch'en and the Development of Early Sung Poetry* (Columbia Univ. Pr., 1976).

Meng Chiao: Stephen Owen, *The Poetry of Meng Chiao and Han Yü* (Yale Univ. Pr., 1975).

Ou-yang Hsiu: James T. C. Liu, *Ou-yang Hsiu: An Eleventh Century Neo-Confucianist* (Stanford Univ. Pr., 1967).

Po Chü-i: *Selected Poems*, trans. Burton Watson (Columbia Univ. Pr., 2000).

Su Tung P'o: *Selected Poems*, trans. Burton Watson (Columbia Univ. Pr., 1965; rev. ed. Copper Canyon, 1994).

Yang Wan-li: *Heaven My Blanket, Earth My Pillow*, trans. Jonathan Chaves (Weatherhill, 1975).

Yüan Hung-tao: *Pilgrim of the Clouds*, trans. Jonathan Chaves (Weatherhill, 1978).

Anthologies and surveys:

Joseph R. Allen, *In the Voice of Others: Chinese Music Bureau Poetry* (Center for Chinese Studies, Univ. of Michigan, 1992).

Anne Birrell, *New Songs from a Jade Terrace* (George Allen & Unwin, 1982).

Kang-i Sun Chang, *Six Dynasties Poetry* (Princeton Univ. Pr. 1986).

J. D. Frodsham and Ch'eng Hsi, *An Anthology of Chinese Verse* (Oxford Univ. Pr., 1967).

A. C. Graham, *Poems of the Late T'ang* (Penguin, 1965).

Shuen-fu Lin, *The Transformation of the Chinese Lyrical Tradition* (Princeton Univ. Pr., 1978).

—— & Stephen Owen, eds., *The Vitality of the Lyric Voice* (Princeton Univ. Pr., 1986).

Victor H. Mair, ed., *The Columbia History of Chinese Literature* (Columbia Univ. Pr., 2001).

Stephen Owen, *The Great Age of Chinese Poetry* (Yale Univ. Pr., 1981).

——, *The Poetry of the Early T'ang* (Yale Univ. Pr., 1977).

Stephen C. Soong, ed., *A Brotherhood of Song: Chinese Poetry and Poetics* (Chinese Univ. Pr., Hong Kong, 1985).

——, ed., *Song Without Music: Chinese Tz'u Poetry* (Chinese Univ. Pr., Hong Kong, 1980).

Burton Watson, *Chinese Lyricism* (Columbia Univ. Pr., 1971).

Kojiro Yoshikawa, *An Introduction to Sung Poetry*, trans. Burton Watson (Harvard Univ. Pr., 1967).

Pauline Yu, ed., *Voices of the Song Lyric in China* (Univ. of California Pr., 1994).

NOTES

EARLY POETS (TO 618)

SHIH CHING (12th c.–7th c. B.C.E.)

The *Shih Ching* (known in English as *The Book of Odes, The Book of Songs, The Confucian Odes, The Poetry Classic*) is the earliest Chinese anthology. Reputedly compiled by Confucius himself in the 6th century B.C.E., it remained required reading for civil service examinations until the modern era. Its 305 surviving poems include erotic lyrics, liturgical hymns, political protests, fertility songs, ballads of war and disaster, and dynastic histories.

Confucius (*Analects* VII, 9, trans. Fang): "Why don't you study the Odes? The Odes will arouse you, give you food for thought, teach you how to make friends, show you the way of resentment, bring you near to being useful to your parents and sovereign, and help you remember the names of many birds, animals, plants and trees."

Confucius (*Analects* II, 2, trans. EP): "The anthology of 300 poems can be gathered into the one sentence: Have no twisty thoughts."

Meng Chiao: "I've spent my whole life writing a thousand poems that just copy the Odes."

p. 3, SONG OF THE BOWMEN OF SHU: WCW (from *Spring and All*, V, 1923):

> Black wind, I have poured my heart out
> to you until I am sick of it—
>
> Now I run my hand over you feeling
> the play of your body—the quiver
> of its strength—
>
> The grief of the bowmen of Shu
> moves nearer—There is
> an approach with difficulty from
> the dead—the winter casing of grief
>
> How easy to slip
> into the old mode, how hard to
> cling firmly to the advance—

p.5, "PINE BOAT A-SHIFT": We can follow EP's method of translating the *Odes* by looking at the sources he used: James Legge's 1876 *The She King* and the Swedish Sinologist Bernard Karlgren's 1950 *The Book of Odes*, which had the Chinese text, transliterations (including reconstructions of the archaic pronunciations for the rhyme-words), and a prose translation. EP never mentioned, but probably also used Arthur Waley's 1937 version, *The Book of Songs*.

The famous first stanza of EP's version is, in Legge:

> It floats about, that boat of cypress wood,
> Now here, now there, as by the current borne.
> Nor rest nor sleep comes in my troubled mood;
> I suffer as when painful has torn
> The shrinking body.   Thus I dwell forlorn,
> And aimless muse, my thoughts of sorrow full.
> I might with wine refresh my spirit worn;
> I might go forth, and sauntering try to cool
> The fever of my heart; but grief holds sullen rule.

In Karlgren:

> Drifting is that cypress-wood boat, drifting is its floating [So I am drifting helplessly along, without means of steering my way]; I am [bright=] wide awake and do not sleep, as if I had a painful grief; but it is not that I have no wine, to amuse and divert myself.

For the third line, EP takes the components of the character *keng* (bright/awake),"ear" and "fire," sees in Matthews' dictionary of modern usage (Achilles Fang: "Would you use Webster's Collegiate Dictionary to translate Chaucer?") that *keng* also means "disquieted," and produces "flame in the ear, sleep riven." For the fourth line (literally, "like having hidden sorrow") he sees the "heart" radical in the last two characters, and writes: "driven; rift of the heart in dark." And for the sixth line, he may have found "play" in Waley:

> Tossed is that cypress boat,
> Wave-tossed it floats.
> My heart is in turmoil, I cannot sleep.
> But secret is my grief.
> Wine I have, all things needful
> For play, for sport.

p. 8, "WITHERED, WITHERED, BY THE WIND'S OMEN": EP note: "*Where the winds blow, withered leaves must. / Folk under overlords are as blown dust.* L[egge] and K[arlgren] completely at loggerheads. Following Mao [the standard text in Chinese] the meaning would be: The prince, overborne by his ministers, ironizes."

p. 8, "WIDE, HO?": EP note: "Said to be by the divorced wife of Huan of Sung, after her son's accession, decorum forbidding her to return to court."

p. 10, "SOFT WIND OF THE VALE": EP title: "East Wind."

p. 11, "FLUID AS WATER THAT ALL TONES REFLECTS": EP note: "On Yüan hill, mutable, affable, candid, but held of no account."

p. 12, "A BOAT FLOATS OVER SHADOW": EP note: "Rumours as to the death of Süan's sons."

CH'Ü YÜAN (*c.* 340–278 B.C.E.)

The first major Chinese poet known by name, he was an official who was undone by intrigues in the court, and drowned himself in the Mi-lou River. The Dragon-Boat Festival is celebrated on the fifth day of the fifth month in his honor: people go out in boats to look for his body.

Chinese poetry begins with, and is always returning to, two anthologies: the *Odes* and the *Ch'u Tz'u* (usually known in English as the *Songs of the South*), written by Ch'ü Yüan and his followers. The two couldn't be more different: South to the *Odes'* North, the *Ch'u Tz'u* contains, among other things, long, first-person dreamlike narratives (most notably, the *Li Sao*, "Encountering Sorrow"); a long poem consisting entirely of cosmological questions (the *Tian Wen*, "Heaven Questions"); and the "Nine Songs" (there are eleven), which are based on aboriginal shamanic chants. Surprisingly, with the exception of this fragment by EP, the *Ch'u Tz'u* poems have attracted scholars but not poets. Among them, Arthur Waley translated the "Nine Songs"; Stephen Field the *Tian Wen* (New Directions, 1986); and David Hawkes the whole book.

p. 17, AFTER CHU YUAN: From one of the "Nine Songs." A pre-*Cathay* translation, first published (with Liu Ch'e and Pan Chieh-yü, below) in the 1914 *Des Imagistes* anthology. EP's half-Chinese, half-Dionysian translation was carved out of a prolix prose version in Herbert Giles' 1901 *History of Chinese Literature*. Its first of five paragraphs reads: "Methinks there is a Genius of the hills, clad in wistaria, girdled with ivy, with smiling lips, of witching mien, riding on the red pard, wild cats galloping in the rear, reclining in a chariot, with banners of cassia, cloaked with the orchid, girt with azalea, culling the perfume of sweet flowers to leave behind a memory in the heart. But dark is the grove wherein I dwell. No light of day reaches it ever. The path thither is dangerous and difficult to climb. Alone I stand on the hill-top, while the clouds float beneath my feet, and all around is wrapped in gloom."

LIU CH'E (EMPEROR WU OF THE HAN) (156–87 B.C.E.)

The sixth emperor of the Han and an extravagant patron of the arts. The *fu* (rhyme-prose) form was invented at his court, which also included the great historian Ssu-ma Ch'ien. He expanded the obscure Music Bureau (*Yüeh-fu*) into a large bureaucracy employing over eight hundred people; their task was to collect folk songs as a way of knowing what the people were thinking, and to create songs and poetry for the sacrifices and rites. *Yüeh-fu* became the name of a genre that remained popular for centuries: a kind of pseudo-folk song composed by poets. During the T'ang, *yüeh-fu* poems of political protest were often set in the reign of Wu to make the criticism indirect.

p. 18, LIU CH'E: Like Ch'ü Yüan, above, a pre-*Cathay* "Imagiste" poem, remarkably extracted from the following by Giles:

> The sound of rustling is stilled,
> With dust the marble courtyard filled;
> No footfalls echo on the floor,
> Fallen leaves in heaps block up the door . . .
> For she, my pride, my lovely one, is lost,
> And I am left, in hopeless anger tossed.

[Author's ellipsis.] The last word of the first line in EP's translation was originally "del-icate," but Richard Aldington had recently been parodying EP's overuse of the word. EP changed it to "elaborate," which his future wife Dorothy Shakespear found "rococo & heavy." She suggested "discontinued"; thus, one of the most famous lines in *Cathay*. The last line was EP's Imagist invention, or intervention.

EP, ever on the lookout for enlightened rulers, declared in 1914 (on the basis of a few poems in Giles) that Liu Ch'e and the Greek poet Ibycus were the quintessential Imagists, and, in 1915, that the poems of Liu Ch'e and a few others would be as great a stimulus to the 21st century as the Greeks were to the Renaissance.

CHO WEN-CHÜN (c. 150–115 B.C.E.)

KR (*Orchid*): "One of the most famous lovers in Chinese history. The daughter of a wealthy man in Szechuan, she was widowed at seventeen, whereupon Ssu-ma Hsiang-ju, a poor writer, fell in love with her. He played the psaltery and sang to her at a banquet given by her father and she eloped with him. Disowned and poverty-stricken, they opened a wine shop. This so humiliated her father that he gave them a large sum of money. Ssu-ma Hsiang-ju became famous, the leading court poet of the Emperor Wu of the Han and took a concubine. Broken-hearted, Cho Wen-chün wrote ["Lament"], which so moved her husband that he gave up the concubine and returned to her. This story is probably pure legend. In many collections the poem is anonymous."

p. 19, LAMENT OF A GRAYING WOMAN: Also translated by KR in *Orchid* as "A Song of White Hair" under the name Chuo Wen-chün.

PAN CHIEH-YÜ (LADY PAN) (c. 48 B.C.E.)

KR (*Love*): "She was a favorite concubine of the Emperor Ch'eng Ti of the Han. Discarded by him, she wrote one of the first and best 'deserted courtesan' poems, which would be imitated innumerable times in the centuries to come."

She is the subject of a famous 4th-century painting by Ku K'ai-chih in the British Museum, stolen from the Imperial Palace in Peking during the Boxer Rebellion, and undoubtedly known to EP.

p. 20, FAN-PIECE, FOR HER IMPERIAL LORD: A pre-*Cathay*, "Imagiste" translation, like Ch'ü Yüan and Liu Ch'e above, condensed from a version in Giles' 1901 *History*. In this case, EP fashioned a haiku out of:

> O fair white silk, fresh from the weaver's loom,
> Clear as the frost, bright as the winter snow—
> See! friendship fashions out of thee a fan,
> Round as the round moon shines in heaven above,
> At home, abroad, a close companion thou,
> Stirring at every move the grateful gale.
> And yet I fear, ah me! that autumn chills,
> Cooling the dying summer's torrid rage,
> Will see thee laid neglected on the shelf,
> All thoughts of bygone days, like them bygone.

p. 20, A PRESENT FROM THE EMPEROR'S NEW CONCUBINE: From *Love*; later retranslated by KR as "A Song of Grief" in *Orchid*.

ANONYMOUS (HAN DYNASTY, 206 B.C.E.–220 C.E.)

p. 21, A BALLAD OF THE MULBERRY ROAD: A *yüeh-fu*, *circa* 1st century C.E. Here, the story goes that the Ch'in (EP: Shin) family had a married daughter named Lo-fu (EP: Rafu). When she went to gather mulberries by the side of the road, the King of Chao saw her from a tower and invited her to drink wine. But Lo-fu was a skilled musician, so she composed this ballad to tell him how she felt, and the King gave up his attempt at seduction. EP translates only the beginning of the poem.

p. 21, THE BEAUTIFUL TOILET: EP note: "By Mei Sheng, B.C. 140." No longer attributed to Mei Sheng, the poem is one of the "Nineteen Old Poems," probably composed in the 1st century C.E. Somewhere between *yüeh-fu* folk songs and literary poems, they introduced the five-character line to Chinese poetry, and remained popular and influential for many centuries.

p. 22, "She weaves and ends no pattern to day": Another of the "Nineteen Old Poems." The Weaving Girl and the Ox-herding Boy are the stars Altair and Vega, estranged lovers who once a year (on the 7/7 festival) cross the Han River (the Milky Way) and meet.

EP, in the late 1950s, after his release from St. Elizabeths, returned to the Fenollosa manuscripts and wrote these two versions, probably his last Chinese translations. He titled them "Baijo's Poem in the Koshigen." Baijo is the Japanese pronunciation of Mei Sheng (see above); the *Koshigen* is the *Ku-shih Yüan* ("The Origins of Verse"), a 14-volume anthology of pre-T'ang poetry compiled in 1719 by Shen Te-ch'ien. Along with the poems, EP wrote:

> At a time when academic persons are being subsidized to write about Fenollosa's influence, it might be permitted, not to wail, but to note with perhaps a touch of asperity, that apart from the first $200 Mrs Fenollosa dug, I believe, out of someone in Canada, the editing of Fenollosa's papers was at my own cost and charge and the returns would not have paid a typist to make copies. The *Written Character* was abbreviated to get it printed at all [. . .]. In fact I could a hell derive from various obstructors of learning. I emphasized the points least known to the English-reading public, but that did not in intention imply Fenollosa's ignorance of other items known even to the best paid and stupidest sinologues. [. . .] My own ignorance of the simplest matters was gradually and partially diminished. On return from incarceration I had the strength to tackle a few more pages of our author's not over legible penciling, from which the following items may serve.

LU CHI (261–303)

See note under "On Chinese Poetry," below, p. 240.

T'AO CH'IEN (365–427)

His given name was T'ao Yüan-ming; "Ch'ien" means "recluse." The first Ch'an Buddhist poet, though he lived outside of the monastery, the first to describe ordinary experience in plain speech, the father of "fields and gardens" poetry (as Hsieh Ling-yün is the father of "rivers and mountains" poetry), he was more or less forgotten until he was enthusiastically rediscovered in the T'ang by Wang Wei, Tu Fu, Li Po, and others. His one-page autobiography reads:

> No one knows where he came from. His given and literary names are also a mystery. But we know there were five willows growing beside his house, which is why he used the name Master Five-Willows. At peace in idleness, rarely speaking, he had no longing for fame or fortune. He loved to read books, and yet never puzzled over their profound insights. But whenever he came upon some realization, he was so pleased that he forgot to eat.
>
> He was a wine-lover by nature, but couldn't afford it very often. Everyone knew this, so when they had wine, they'd call him over. And when he drank, it was always bottoms-up. He'd be drunk in no time; then he'd go back home, alone and with no regrets over where things were going.
>
> In the loneliness of his meager wall, there was little shelter from wind and sun. His short coat was patched and sewn. And made from gourd and split bamboo, his cup and bowl were often empty. But he kept writing poems to amuse himself, and they show something of who he was. He went on like this, forgetting all gain and loss, until he came naturally to his end.
>
> . . . Ch'ien Lou said: "Don't make yourself miserable agonizing over impoverished obscurity, and don't wear yourself out scrambling for money and honor." Doesn't that describe this kind of man perfectly? He'd just get merrily drunk and write poems to cheer himself up. He must have lived in the most enlightened and ancient of times. . . (trans. DH)

Lu Yu (trans. Burton Watson):

> Mist-veiled plants in the little garden reach to the house next door;
> Mulberry trees take deep shade, one small path slanting through.
> I lie down to read T'ao's poems—less than one chapter,
> When fine rain brings an excuse to jump and hoe the melons.

GS (in *Left Out in the Rain*, 1986):

AFTER T'AO CH'IEN

> "Swiftly the years, beyond recall:
> Solemn the stillness of this Spring morning."
> I'll put on my boots & old levis
> & hike across Tamalpais.
> Along the coast the fog hovers,
> Hovers an hour, then scatters.
> There comes a wind, blowing from the sea,
> That brushes the hills of spring grass.

p. 24, TO-EM-MEI'S "THE UNMOVING CLOUD": *To-Em-Mei*: Japanese pronunciation of T'ao Ch'ien.

p. 29, PEACH-BLOSSOM SPRING: See note to Wang Wei.

p. 32, ELEGY FOR MYSELF: "There was a series of twelve standard pitch-pipes used in ancient music, and each pitch corresponded to one of the twelve months. *Wu-yi* corresponds to the 9th lunar month, or October. *Huan T'ui* had such an extravagant coffin made for himself that it took over three years to build. *Yang Wang-sun* (1st c. B.C.E.) insisted on being buried naked so he could return to his true (natural) state." (DH, *T'ao*)

HSIEH LING-YÜN (385–433)

See GS essay, "Hsieh's Shoes," p. 201.

KR (*Love*): "Although his reputation is based upon his nature poetry, meditative elegiac verse describing mountain hermitages, monasteries, or lonely travel, of a type that would have a great influence on Tu Fu, he was actually the proprietor of an immense estate where his fantastic landscaping–at the expense of hundreds of forced laborers–made him enemies in all the surrounding country. He seems to have been restless there, unable to let politics alone, however much he objected to it. Eventually he was demoted from high office and sent to Canton where again he made enemies and finally was executed. He was apparently a rather manic individual and never at rest even at his elaborate retreat. . . . His poetry is remarkable for its dramatic sonority, rather as if Wordsworth had been rewritten by Marlowe. . . . Although Hsieh's verse for his day was extremely modern, even modernistic, there is also something archaizing about it."

DH (*Hsieh*): "[He initiated] a tradition of 'rivers-and-mountains' (*shan-shui*) poetry that stretches across millennia. Fundamentally different from writing that uses the 'natural world' as the stage or materials for human concerns, Hsieh's rivers-and-mountains poetry might best be described as wilderness poetry, poetry that engages or celebrates wilderness of itself and our integral spiritual relationship to it. It invests realistic descriptions of landscape with the philosophy of Taoism and Buddhism, thereby shaping landscape into forms of enlightenment."

T'ao Hung-ching, Taoist hermit (452–536): "Men have always spoken and will always speak of the beauty of mountains and streams. High peaks that go soaring into the clouds; translucent torrents, clear to their very bottoms, flanked on either side by cliffs of stone, whose five-fold colors glitter in the sun; green forests and bamboos of kingfisher-blue, verdant through every season of the year. As the mists of dawn roll aside, the birds and monkeys cry discordantly. As the evening sun sinks to rest, the fishes vie at leaping from their deep pools. Here is the true Paradise of the Region of Earthly Desires. Yet, since the time of Hsieh Ling-yün, no one has been able to feel at one with the these wonders, as he did." (trans. J. D. Frodsham)

p. 36, DWELLING IN THE MOUNTAINS: Ellipses indicate lacunae in the original text.

ANONYMOUS (SIX DYNASTIES, 222–589)

The Southern Six Dynasties *yüeh-fu* are always characterized as "languid and erotic." They were attributed to legendary women, usually courtesans. In the 4th century, the most famous of them, Tzu-yeh, appeared as a ghost, 600 years after her death, and sang her songs to one Wang K'o-chih, who wrote them down.

T'ANG POETS (618–907)

HAN-SHAN (DATE UNKNOWN)

GS (*Riprap*): "Han-shan, 'Cold Mountain,' takes his name from where he lived. He is a mountain madman in an old Chinese line of ragged hermits. His poems, of which 300 survive, are written in T'ang colloquial: rough and fresh. The ideas are Taoist, Buddhist, Zen. He and his sidekick Shih-te became great favorites with Zen painters of later days—the scroll, the broom, the wild hair and laughter. They became Immortals and you sometimes run into them today in the skidrows, orchards, hobo jungles, and logging camps of America."

GS (comments at "Chinese Poetry" symposium): "That fall [1949] . . . I went back to work in a graduate seminar with Ch'en Shih-hsiang. . . . He asked me what I would like to do. I said I would like to do some Buddhist poems that possibly were in a vernacular, and he said 'Of course, Han-shan is the poet you should work with.' In getting into the Han-shan poems, however, I found something that I had not suspected. Prior to that I had translated some T'ang poems as part of class work. Something happened to me that I had not experienced before in the effort of translation, and that was that I found myself forgetting the Chinese and going into a deep interior visualization of what the poem was about. . . . I had just been a four month's season in the high country of the Sierra Nevada, totally out of touch, supplied every two weeks by a packstring that dropped with groceries, and then left alone to work with rocks, picks, dynamite, and a couple of old men who really knew how to do rockwork and an Indian who was a cook. So when I came back, I was still full of that; and when I went into the Han-shan poems, when he talked about a cobbly stream, or he talked about the pine-wind, I wasn't just thinking about 'pine-wind' in Chinese and then 'pine-wind' in English, but I was hearing it, hearing the wind. And when a phrase like 'cloudy mist' or 'misty mountain' or 'cloudy mountain' or 'mountain in the cloud' comes up . . . the strategy ultimately is this: You know the words . . . in the original text, so drop them and now remember what it looks like to look at cloudy mountains and see what they look like, in your mind—go deep into your mind and see what's happening: an interior visualization of the poem, which means of course that you have to draw on your senses, your recollection of your senses. And it certainly helps if you've had some sensory experiences in your life, to have that deep storehouse to pull it out of and re-experience it from, or if you can't re-experience it, go out and look at it again."

LU CHAO-LIN (634–c. 684)

A crippled erudite and alchemist, author of the famous "Rhyme-prose on the Diseased Pear Tree," he called himself the Master of Shrouded Sorrow, spent his last years experimenting with drugs, and drowned himself in the river Ying.

p. 58, OLD IDEA OF CHOAN: EP translates only the first sixteen of the poem's 68 lines. Choan = Ch'ang-an. Butei of Kan = the Emperor Han.

HO CHIH-CHANG (659–744)

An obscure poet, friend of Li Po's, known for this one poem. [In KR (*Love*) as Ho Ch'e Chang.]

MENG HAO-JAN (689–740)

KR (*Love*): "His middle years were spent as a hermit in the mountains. He is famous for having hidden under Wang Wei's bed when the Emperor Hsuan Tsung came to call. Having offended the Emperor, he was not given a post and went happily back to his hermitage." (The story is probably untrue. Meng lived as a recluse, then at age 40 decided to go to the capital to take the examinations to become a civil servant. He failed, and returned to the mountains.)

DH (*Mountain*): "A major catalyst in the T'ang renaissance was admiration for T'ao Ch'ien and Hsieh Ling-yün, who had been neglected since their deaths. During this hiatus, Ch'an Buddhism came to maturity and became widely practiced among the intelligentsia of China. Ch'an not only clarified anew the spiritual ecology of early Taoist thought, it also emphasized the old Taoist idea that deep understanding lies beyond words. In poetry, this gave rise to a much more distilled language, especially in its concise imagism. . . which opened new inner depths, non-verbal insights, and even outright enigma. It was in the work of Meng Hao-jan, the first great T'ang Dynasty poet, that this poetic revolution began. And although later poets developed this new aesthetic further, there is a sense in which Meng remained its most radical exemplar: it is said that he destroyed most poems after writing them because he didn't feel words could capture his intent."

WANG WEI (701–761)

Sometime government official, sometime Ch'an monk, inventor of the landscape scroll painting (only countless imitations of his originals survive), recluse on his family estate along the Wang (Wheel-Rim) River. "Wang Wei is one of those model poets, personally and artistically flawless, who occur very rarely in the history of literature." (KR, *Love*)

KR ("Poetic Landscape"): "Much Far Eastern poetry is concerned with the transitoriness of human values, the ephemeral beauties of nature, the impermanent illusion of the ego, with the life of man as a tiny series of unknown incidents in the flow of the universe. These are Wang Wei's special, characteristic, almost exclusive concerns. Many of his most famous poems are short quatrains, solemn and infinitely suggestive, in which he begins the literary and philosophical tendencies that would culminate in the still more ephemeral and suggestive Japanese haiku. In fact, several Japanese haiku are simply compressions of quatrains by Wang Wei."

EP (letter, 1916): "I have spent the day with Wang Wei, eighth century Jules Laforgue Chinois." EP (letter, 1917): "[Wang Wei] is the real modern–even Parisian–of VIII cent. China."

The lines in EP's Canto IV:

> Smoke hangs on the stream,
> The peach-trees shed bright leaves in the water,
> Sound drifts in the evening haze,
> The bark scrapes at the ford,

> Gilt rafters above black water,
> > Three steps in an open field,
> Gray stone posts leading. . .

are drawn from Fenollosa's translation of Wang Wei's poem, "Peach Source Spring," itself a version of T'ao Ch'ien's "Peach Blossom Spring" (p. 29). It is known that Pound translated the Wang Wei poem, but it was never published and the manuscript has disappeared. T'ao Ch'ien's tale of paradise appears near the end of the *Pisan Cantos*.

Su Tung-p'o: "There is poetry in his painting and painting in his poetry."

Wang Wei (letter): "Without the animation of feelings of grief, one's style flows lightly and is insipid."

LI PO (701–762)

DH (*Li Po*): "As with most immortals, the facts of Li Po's existence are nebulous. He was himself the ultimate source for most of the biographical information we have, and with his perpetual self-dramatization, he was a decidedly unreliable source."

He was (or wasn't) a Central Asian—perhaps not Chinese at all—who claimed direct descent from the (probably mythic) Lao Tzu; a Taoist recluse; a freelance avenging angel, killing those who had brought suffering to the poor; a court poet in Ch'ang-an, who amused the capital with his eccentricities; a wanderer in the fringes of the empire; a prisoner and an exile in the chaos of the An Lu-shan rebellion; the archetypal Chinese poet who–the legend goes–drowned when, drunk in a boat, he tried to embrace the reflection of the moon. He and his friend Tu Fu are traditionally considered the two greatest Chinese poets, and the two poles of Chinese poetry, with Li Po the Dionysian-Taoist and Tu Fu the Apollonian-Confucian. Most of Li Po's work is lost, and many of the remaining thousand poems attributed to him are dubious.

Tu Fu: "For Li Po, it's a hundred poems per gallon of wine."

WCW (Prologue to *Kora in Hell*, 1918): "Li Po is reported to have written his best verse supported in the arms of the Emperor's attendants and with a dancing girl to hold his tablet. He was also a great poet."

WCW (letter to EP, 1933): "Fer the luv of God snap out of it. I'm no more sentimental about 'murika' than Li Po was about China or Shakespeare about Yingland or any damned Frog about Paris."

WCW (letter to Robert Lowell, 1947): "Li Po can be imitated not with the synthetic moons we have about us nowadays."

KR (from "August 22, 1939," *In What Hour*, 1940):

> What is it all for, this poetry,
> This bundle of accomplishment
> Put together with so much pain?
> Twenty years at hard labor,
> Lessons learned from Li Po and Dante,
> Indian chants and gestalt psychology;
> What words can it spell,
> This alphabet of one sensibility?

p. 73, The River-Merchant's Wife: A Letter: "Perhaps the most interesting form of modern poetry is to be found in Browning's 'Men and Women.' This kind of poem, which reaches its climax in his unreadable 'Sordello'. . . has had a curious history in the west. You may say it begins in Ovid's 'Heroides,' which purport to be letters written between Helen and Paris or by Enone and other distinguished persons of classical pseudo-history; or you may find an earlier example in Theocritus' Idyl of the woman spinning at her sombre and magical wheel. From Ovid to Browning this sort of poem was very much neglected. It is interesting to find, in eighth-century China, a poem which might have been slipped into Browning's work without causing any surprise save by its simplicity and naive beauty." (EP, "Chinese Poetry")

"The poetry of great quality is that without comment as without effort it presents you with images that stir your emotions; so you are made a better man; you are softened, rendered more supple of mind, more open to the vicissitudes and necessities of your fellow men. When you have read 'The River-Merchant's Wife' you are added to. You are a better man or woman than you were before." (Ford Maddox Ford, "Ezra," 1927)

"'The River-Merchant's Wife' is a modernist classic. . . . Nevertheless, there is no reason to think the husband is a river-merchant. The wandering Li Po was likely thinking figuratively of his own wife." (DH, *Li Po*)

p. 77, The Jewel Stairs' Grievance: EP's famous note to this poem in *Cathay* is abridged from the following in the uncollected essay "Chinese Poetry":

> I have never found any occidental who could "make much" of that poem at one reading. Yet upon careful examination we find that everything is there, not merely by "suggestion" but by a sort of mathematical process of reduction. Let us consider what circumstances would be needed to produce just the words of this poem. You can play Conan Doyle if you like.
>
> First, "jewel-stairs," therefore the scene is in a palace.
>
> Second, "gauze stockings," therefore a court lady is speaking, not a servant or common person who is in the palace by chance.
>
> Third, "dew soaks," therefore the lady has been waiting, she has not just come.
>
> Fourth, "clear autumn with moon showing," therefore the man who has not come cannot excuse himself on the grounds that the evening was unfit for the rendezvous.
>
> Fifth, you ask how we know she was waiting for a man? Well, the title calls the poem "grievance," and for that matter, how do we know what she was waiting for?

p. 84, On Phoenix Tower in Chin-ling: "The mythic phoenix appears only in times of peace and sagacious rule, which was certainly not the case during the An Lushan rebellion when this poem was written." (DH, *Li Po*) It is estimated that, during the rebellion, 38 million of China's 53 million people died or became homeless.

p. 86, "The red sun comes out": First half of the poem, translated in its entirety as "Sunflight Chant" in DH, *Li Po*.

p. 89, War South of the Great Wall: "Another kind of *yüeh-fu*, the traditional form for poems of social protest, which allows rather extreme metrical irregularities. As is often the case with T'ang Dynasty *yüeh-fu*, it is set in the Han Dynasty—a convention used when the poem was likely to offend those in power (here the protest would be against the expansionist militarism of the government). The speaker is a soldier." (DH, *Li Po*)

CH'U KUANG-HSI (*fl.* 742)
A minor official in Ch'ang-an; forced to serve the An Lu-shan rebels; imprisoned after the restoration; officially pardoned but banished nevertheless to the south, where he died. [Published in KR, *Love*, under the name Ch'u Chuang I.]

WANG CH'ANG-LING (*c.* 690–*c.* 756)
In his lifetime, the most renowned poet of the T'ang; a minor functionary who was killed sometime during the An Lu-shan rebellion. He wrote that poetry "concentrates the sea of heaven in the inch-space of the heart."

TU FU (712–770)
See KR essay, p. 198.

p. 97, SONG OF THE WAR-CARTS: "There was no compulsory military service. However, press-gangs were used in times of heavy fighting, when there weren't enough volunteers to fill the military's needs. [*Emperor Wu*: See Liu Ch'e, above.] *Sky-Blue Seas*: Koko Nor (Chinghai Hu), a large lake on a plain in the Tibetan highlands. *Weeping of old ghosts*: Until men killed in battle are buried, their spirits linger weeping." (DH, *Tu Fu*)

p. 99, P'ENG-YA SONG: "The poem recounts the flight of Tu Fu's family just after the rebels captured Ch'ang-an. *Summon our souls*: It was generally thought that the soul left the body when a person was surprised or frightened. *Drift away*: It was also thought that in sleep the soul drifted away." (DH, *Tu Fu*)

p. 100, SPRING VIEW: Also translated by DH as "Spring Landscape" in *Tu Fu*.

p. 104, TO WEI PA, A RETIRED SCHOLAR: "Rhinoceros-horn cups didn't hold much liquor." (KR, *100*)

p. 105, FOR THE RECLUSE WEI PA: "*Scorpio and Orion*: One of these constellations sets just before the other rises, so they never 'see' each other." (DH, *Tu Fu*)

p. 106, MOON FESTIVAL: "The Chinese see a toad, a rabbit and a mortar, a tree, and a girl, Chang-O, in the moon, where we see a face." (KR, *100*)

p. 107, TRAVELING NORTHWARD: A five-line excerpt from the long poem, "The Journey North," translated in its entirety in DH, *Tu Fu*.

p. 107, STANDING ALONE: Also translated by KR as "Loneliness" in *100*.

p. 107, LANDSCAPE: Also translated by KR as "Overlooking the Desert" in *100*.

p. 108, TO PI SSU YAO: "Tu Fu means that the poems, as the best possible descendants, will always perform the ancestral rites—the sentiment of Horace and Shakespeare. When no one remained to honor a dead man's tablet, his ghost, to all intents, ceased to exist." (KR, *100*)

p. 112, FULL MOON: Also translated by KR under the same title in *100*.

CH'IEN CH'I (*c. 722–c. 780*)

Director of the Bureau of Evaluations in Ch'ang-an; in his lifetime hailed as the successor to Wang Wei, his friend, but later considered inferior in comparison. One of his best-known poems is "Fleeing in the Night to a Buddhist Temple in the Southern Mountains with Auxiliary Secretary Hsüeh and Wang the Rectifier of Omissions when the Eastern City Walls of Ch'ang-an Began to Fall to the Tibetans."

p. 116, VISIT TO THE HERMIT TS'UI: "[It] is a bread and butter note; the finest such poem is probably the Japanese *waka* echoing Wang Wei: 'Although it was not my own home / The wild plum by the window / Smelled just the same.'" [KR, *Love*]

CHANG CHI (MID-8th c.)

Little is known of his life, and little was thought of his poetry, except for "Maple Bridge," one of the most popular poems in its day and ever since. Not to be confused with Chang Chi, a poet of social realism and political satire from the next generation.

p. 117, MAPLE BRIDGE NIGHT MOORING: GS visited the same bridge in 1984, and wrote this response (in *The Gary Snyder Reader*):

> AT MAPLE BRIDGE
>
> Men are mixing gravel and cement
> At Maple bridge,
> Down an alley by a tea-stall
> From Cold Mountain temple
> Where Chang Chi heard the bell.
> The stone step moorage
> Empty, lapping water,
> And the bell sound has traveled
> Far across the sea.

CHAO LUAN-LUAN (8th c.)

KR (*Orchid*): "She was an elegant prostitute in the pleasure city of Ch'ang An, the T'ang capital. Her poems were a common type, a sort of advertising copy in praise of the parts of a woman's body, written for courtesans and prostitutes."

MENG CHIAO (751–814)

A Ch'an recluse who, at forty, unsuccessfully attempted a career in the bureaucracy, and then lived as an impoverished poet in Lo-yang, the eastern capital. The founder of a radical tradition that would later include Li Ho and Li Shang-yin, whose dark symbolism and Chinese surrealism would not be appreciated until the West discovered the same things a millennium later.

Su Tung-p'o (trans. Burton Watson):

Night: reading Meng Chiao's poems,
characters fine as cow's hair.
By the cold lamp, my eyes blur and swim.
Good passages I rarely find–
lone flowers poking up from the mud–
but more hard words than the *Odes* or *Li sao*–
jumbled rocks clogging the clear stream,
making rapids too swift for poling.

My first impression is of eating little fishes–
what you get's not worth the trouble;
or of boiling tiny mud crabs
and ending up with some empty claws.
For refinement he might compete with monks
but he'll never match his master Han Yü.
Man's life is like morning dew,
a flame eating up the oil night by night.
Why should I strain my ears
listening to the squeaks of this autumn insect?
Better lay aside the book
and drink my cup of jade-white wine.

Meng Chiao: "A poet only suffers writing poems. / Better to spend your time learning how to fly."

p. 120, FROM MOURNING LU YIN: "*Lu Yin*: a minor poet and friend of Meng Chiao's." (DH, *Meng*)

p. 122, LAMENTS OF THE GORGES: "*Gorges*: A 200-mile stretch of very narrow canyons formed where the Yangtze River cuts through the Wu Mountains; also known as the Three Gorges. These dangerous canyons were located on the very outskirts of the civilized world, in a part of south China inhabited primarily by aboriginal peoples, and exiled scholar-officials often traveled downriver through them. They are famous in Chinese poetry (notably Tu Fu's late work) for the river's violence and the towering cliffs alive with shrieking gibbons. *Death-owl's call*: The owl's voice resembles that of a ghost or spirit, so when it calls, it is thought to be calling the spirit of a dying person away." (DH, *Meng*)

PO CHÜ-I (772–846)

See DH essay, p. 213.

KR (*Love*): "More varied in his subject matter than Li Po, Wang Wei, or Tu Fu, he was a master of poignant, unforgettable phrases, many of which could be excerpted and stand alone as separate poems. It is this latter characteristic as much as anything else which accounts for his tremendous popularity with the classical poets of Japan, where, as Arthur Waley points out, he is revered as a god of poetry. He was a great favorite of Waley's, whose translations of Po Chü-i are among the finest poems of the twentieth century, and who also wrote an excellent biography. . . unequaled as an introduction to the T'ang Dynasty."

WCW (poem written *c.* 1920 and unpublished until the manuscript was discovered in the 1980s, now in *Collected Poems, Vol. I*):

TO THE SHADE OF PO CHÜ-I

The work is heavy. I see
bare branches laden with snow.
I try to comfort myself
with thought of your old age.
A girl passes, in a red tam,
the coat above her quick ankles
snow smeared from running and falling—
Of what shall I think now
save of death the bright dancer?

Yang Wan-li: "I've read all the poems of Po and Yüan Chen. All my life I've valued them, but I still don't get the sense: half is about their friends and the other half about private matters."

p. 128, "YIN-YO LAPS IN THE REEDS": An excerpt from "Song of the Lute." For a translation of the complete poem, see Po Chü-i, *Selected Poems*, trans. Burton Watson.

LIU TSUNG-YÜAN (773–819)
A powerful politician at age 32, and then the abdication of the Emperor forced him into exile in the South for most of the rest of his life. "River Snow" is one of the best-known poems in China, and in 1973 Liu was bizarrely promoted as a "materialist" in the Anti-Lin Piao Anti-Confucius Campaign.

CHIA TAO (779–843)
A Ch'an monk who left the order to move to Ch'ang-an, fail the examinations, and become an impoverished poet in the Meng Chiao circle.

DH (*Mountain*): "Chia became legendary for wandering the city lost in imaginative reverie as he tried to hone a perfectly turned phrase or image."

TU MU (803–852)
His grandfather was Prime Minister, but his father lost the family fortune, and Tu Mu grew up in a house deserted by the servants, where possessions were sold off to buy food. He was unlucky in the bureaucracy, always backing the wrong faction in palace disputes, and had the unfortunate habit of writing his superiors to tell them what was wrong with their policies and how his promotion could improve matters.

LI YÜ (937–978)
The Last Emperor of the Southern T'ang, who spent his last three years as a prisoner of the conquering Sung. He is credited with transforming *tz'u*, tea house love songs,

into a high art form. One of his most famous lyrics recalls a favorite concubine "chewing pieces of red silk / and spitting them at her lover with a smile."

SUNG POETS (960–1279)

MEI YAO-CH'EN (1002–1060)

A low-ranking bureaucrat, impoverished author of some 2,800 surviving poems, founder with his friend Ou-yang Hsiu of the new Sung style, with its emphasis on plain speech (after the Baroque excesses of the Late T'ang) and previously unsung subject matter, such as earthworms, rats, maggots, lice, and "On Hearing Some Travelers Speak of Eating River-pig."

Mei Yao-ch'en: "Though the poet may trust to inspiration, it is extremely difficult to choose words correctly. If he manages to use words with a fresh skill and to achieve some effect that no one has ever achieved, then he may consider that he has done well. He must be able to paint some scene that is difficult to depict, in such a way that it seems to be right before the eyes of the reader and has an endless significance that exists outside the words themselves."

KR (from "Mary and the Seasons," *In Defense of the Earth*, 1956):

> The mist turns to rain. We are
> All alone in the forest.
> No one is near us for miles.
> In the firelight mice scurry
> Hunting crumbs. Tree toads cry like
> Tiny owls. Deer snort in the
> Underbrush. Their eyes are green
> In the firelight like balls of
> Foxfire. This morning I read
> Mei Yao Chen's poems. . .

OU-YANG HSIU (1007–1072)

Major figure of his time, the complete Confucian "gentleman": powerful politician; inventor of a new prose style; prolific author of lyrics and rhyme-prose, histories of the T'ang and the Five Dynasties, collections of ancient inscriptions, and treatises on, among other subjects, the classics, political factions, and the cultivation of peonies.

Anecdotes of Poets (18th c.): "In middle age, as Chief Administrator of the Prefecture of Ying, Ou-yang Hsiu called himself Recluse Six-One, because he owned ONE thousand books of rubbings of ancient bronze and stone inscriptions, ONE *wan* (10,000) of other books, ONE chess set, ONE *ch'in*, ONE bottle of wine, and was himself ONE old man, growing old with his five things."

Ou-yang Hsiu: "Although it is difficult to acquire mastery in the art of writing, it is all too easy to be pleased with oneself and writers often succumb. Having achieved some degree of competence, they conclude: 'I have attained genuine knowledge.' Some even go so far as to discard all other matters, concerning themselves with nothing else, and justifying their behavior by saying 'I am a writer and my sole job is to write well.'"

p.147, READING THE POEMS OF AN ABSENT FRIEND: "The absent friend is Mei Yao-ch'en. *Aware of the music of verse*: literally, 'the Shao music,' which so entranced Confucius he could not eat meat for three months. A lot of nonsense, following the classical authors, is written about the disappearance of the ancient music in the 'burning of books'– the musical idiom of a people is extraordinarily resistant to change." (KR, *100*)

p. 149, GREEN JADE PLUM TREES IN SPRING: "These poems cannot be appreciated fully unless it is realized that East Wind, plum blossoms, warm mist, and so forth, are mild sexual symbols. Ou Yang-hsiu is a master, along with other virtues, of a quiet eroticism, dreamy as a Sung painting of plum blossoms in mist." (KR, *100*)

SU T'UNG-PO (SU SHIH) (1037–1101)

See GS essay, "Distant Hills," p. 206.

KR (*100*): "He is certainly one of the ten greatest Chinese poets. His work may be full of quotations and allusions to T'ang poetry, T'ao Ch'ien and the classics, but it is still intensely personal and is the climax of early Sung subjectivity. His world is not Tu Fu's. Where the latter sees definite particulars, clear moral issues, bright sharp images, Su Tung-p'o's vision is clouded with the all-dissolving systematic doubt of Buddhism and the nihilism of revived philosophical Taoism. It is a less precise world, but a vaster one, and more like our own."

GS (from "The Canyon Wren," *Mountains and Rivers Without End*, 1996):

> Shooting the Hundred-Pace Rapids
> Su Tung-p'o saw, for a moment,
> it all stand still.
> "I stare at the water:
> it moves with unspeakable slowness."

GS (from "We Wash Our Bowls in This Water," *Mountains and Rivers Without End*):

Su Tung-p'o sat out one whole night by a creek   on the slopes of Mt. Lu. Next morning he showed this poem to his teacher:

> The stream with its sounds   is a long broad tongue
> The looming mountain   is a wide-awake body
> Throughout the night   song after song
> How can I   speak at dawn.

Old Master Chang-tsung approved him.

Su Tung-p'o: "My writings are like the waters of an inexhaustible spring which spread out everywhere over the land. Along the level ground they surge and billow, flowing with ease a thousand *li* in a single day. And when they encounter hills and boulders, bends and turns, they take form from the things about them, though I do not know how they do it. All I know is that they always go where they should go, and stop where they should stop, that is all. Beyond that, even I do not understand." (trans. Burton Watson)

p. 151, THE RED CLIFF: Also translated by DH as "Thinking of Ancient Times at Red Cliffs" in *Mountain*.

p. 152, AT GOLD HILL MONASTERY: "The Scots call this flicker of herring 'keething.' The scene is the mouth of the Yangtze." (KR, *100*)

p. 155, THE TERRACE IN THE SNOW: "I know of few poems which handle so successfully so many dramatic changes of mood." (KR, *100*)

p. 158, THOUGHTS IN EXILE: "The dreamy cities and hill-fringed lakes of Wu, portrayed in countless paintings and sung in innumerable poems, were the very heart of Sung civilization, especially after the loss of North China. Nothing has ever been like it in the West, except possibly Tiepolo's Venice, or somnambulist Paris from the Commune to August 1914." (KR, *100*)

CHU SHU-CHEN (11th c.)

KR (*Orchid*): "Although she has often been ranked as second only to Li Ch'ing-chao, almost nothing is known with certainty of her life, and all the details of her traditional biography, which seems to have been developed largely from her poems, have been questioned."

KR (*Love*): "[Chu and Li] are sisters of Christine de Pisan, Gaspara Stampa, and Louise Labé. There has been no writer like them in English, although a similar sensibility is found, in religious form, in Christina Rossetti."

LI CH'ING-CHAO (c. 1084–c. 1151)

KR (*Orchid*): "She is universally considered to be China's greatest woman poet. She and her husband Chao Ming-ch'eng came from well-known families of scholars and officials. Li's mother had some reputation as a poet, and her father was a friend of Su Tung-p'o's. Li and Chao were an ideal literary couple. They had poetry contests with each other and with their literary friends. They were not only poets but scholars and collectors and spent most of their money to build up a vast collection of seals, bronzes, manuscripts, calligraphy and paintings, and compiled the best critical study and anthology of seals and bronze characters ever written. When in 1127 the army of Chin Tatars invaded Sung China, they were driven from their home and lost most of their collection. In 1129 when Li was forty-six, her husband went alone to a new official post and was taken ill on the way. Li hastened to him, but he died at an inn shortly after she reached him. After her husband's death she lived alone, usually in flight, striving to save what was left of their collection while the Chin were driving the Sung out of North China. Her work is not to be confused with the formularized, deserted-courtesan and abandoned-wife poems so common in Chinese poetry, and usually written by men–for instance, Li Po's 'The Jewel Stairs' Grievance.' Her poems are truly personal utterances, and they fall into three groups: the period of happily married life; that of desolation at the death of her husband; and that of increasing loneliness as she grew old."

p. 162, SORROW OF DEPARTURE: Earlier version by KR in *100*: "To the Tune, 'Plum Blossoms Fall and Scatter.'"

p. 163, FADING PLUM BLOSSOMS: Referring to another poem of hers, Li Ch'ing-chao wrote: "Poets in the past always complained that to write about plum blossoms was very difficult, for you can hardly avoid vulgarism. Now that I have tried it, I totally agree with them."

p. 164, AUTUMN LOVE: Earlier version by KR in *Love*: "A Weary Song to a Slow Sad Tune."

p. 167, ON SPRING: Earlier version by KR in *100*: "Mist."

p. 168, A SONG OF DEPARTURE: Earlier versions by KR in *100* ("Alone in the Night") and *Orchid* ("The Sorrow of Departure").

p. 169, SPRING ENDS: Earlier versions by KR in *Love* ("To the Tune 'Spring at Wu Ling'") and *Orchid* ("Spring Ends").

LU YU (1125–1210)

KR (*Love*): "Lu Yu is the least classical of the major Sung poets. Although a member of the scholar gentry, he never attained, or desired, high office, and seems to have been genuinely far from rich, especially toward the end of his life. (Understand that throughout China's history a really 'poor farmer' never got a chance to read or write anything.) His poetry is loose, casual. It had to be–he wrote about eleven thousand poems. His poems have that easy directness that is supposed to come only with rare, concentrated effort. By his day Sung China had retreated to the South and the Golden Tatars in the North were already being threatened by the Mongols who were soon to overwhelm all. Lu Yu's patriotism was not prepared to accept the *modus vivendi* less doctrinaire minds had worked out, and his stirring agitational poems against the invader have been very popular in twentieth-century China where everybody has been an invader to everybody else."

Lu Yu: "We make our poems out of pure sadness, for without sadness how would we have any poems?"

Tai Fu-ku (1167–?) on Lu Yu: "Using what is plain and simple he fashioned subtle lines; / Taking the most ordinary words, he changed them into wonders." (trans. Burton Watson)

p. 176, THE WILD FLOWER MAN: "There is a veiled ironic reference to a Sung Buddhist saint who was reputed to live only on honey." (KR, *100*)

YANG WAN-LI (1127–1206)

An important official who fell in and out of favor; a devout Buddhist who developed a Ch'an theory of poetic careers: in the disciple stage, one imitates the masters; then one achieves a poetic "enlightenment" and effortlessly writes one's own poetry. His poem on a fly is thought to be the first in Chinese.

DH (*Mountain*): "Yang Wan-li was the last of the great Sung poets, and with him China's rivers-and-mountains poetry had opened up virtually all of its possibilities. China's poets would continue to actively cultivate this rich terrain up to the present, but there would be few really fundamental innovations."

Yang Wan-li (trans. Jonathan Chaves):

> I don't feel like reading another book,
> and I'm tired of poetry—that's not what I want to do.
> But my mind is restless, unsettled—
> I'll try counting raindrop stains
>   on the oilcloth window.

HSIN CH'I-CHI (1140–1207)
Military general, provincial governor, and "pacification commissioner," friend of Lu Yu, he wrote 1,626 surviving *tz'u*, set to 110 different melodies, as well as 120 other poems.

CHIANG CHIEH (1245–c. 1310)
A minor functionary who, after the fall of the Sung, refused to serve the conquering Mongols and became a hermit. Only a hundred of his poems survive because, in the 19th century, a group of young poets who were ardent fans destroyed all the poems they considered inferior.

ON CHINESE POETRY

LU CHI
[Achilles Fang was born to a Chinese family in Japanese-occupied Korea in 1910. He went to China as a student and remained until after the Second World War, collecting books, teaching German, Latin, and Greek, and editing the journal *Monumenta Serica*. In 1947, he moved to the U.S. to work on a Chinese-English dictionary project at Harvard, but was fired for embedding too many quotations from *Finnegans Wake* in the entries. He earned a Ph.D. there, writing an 865-page dissertation on the sources of the *Cantos*, which he refused to publish, and stayed on to teach until his retirement. During the St. Elizabeths years, Fang was Pound's main interlocutor on things Chinese. His personal library was legendary and it was said that he knew everything, but he published little: some arcane and idiosyncratic scholarly articles; an introduction to Pound's *Confucian Odes*; two volumes of a heavily annotated, unfinished translation of *The Chronicle of Three Kingdoms*; and a few miscellaneous translations. He died in 1995.]

Fang: "Lu Chi was China's first articulate literary critic, and one of its greatest. He was born in 261 in the kingdom of Wu, where the Lu clan enjoyed the confidence of the Royal House. After the kingdom was conquered by the Chin, Lu Chi and his brother Lu Yün crossed the Yangtze to try their fortune in the northern capital. He was too scintillating for the comfort of his jealous contemporaries; in 303 he, along with his two brothers and two sons, was put to death on a false charge of high treason. A powerful poet and a writer of spirited prose, his literary reputation has never waned, for he was one of the "inventors" in the Poundian sense. The *Wen-fu* is considered one of the most articulate treatises on Chinese poetics. The extent of its influence in Chinese literary history is equaled only by that of the sixth-century *The Literary Mind and the Carving of Dragons* of Liu Hsieh. In the original, the *Wen-fu* is rhymed, but does not employ regular rhythmic patterns: hence the term 'rhymeprose.'"

GS (from "Axe Handles," in *Axe Handles*, 1983):

> There I begin to shape the old handle
> With the hatchet, and the phrase
> First learned from Ezra Pound
> Rings in my ears!
> "When making an axe handle
>   the pattern is not far off."
> And I say this to Kai
> "Look: We'll shape the handle
> By checking the handle
> Of the axe we cut with—"
> And he sees. And I hear it again:
> It's in Lu Ji's *Wen Fu*, fourth century
> A.D. "Essay on Literature"—in the
> Preface: "In making the handle
> Of an axe
> By cutting wood with an axe
> The model is indeed near at hand."
> My teacher Shih-hsiang Chen
> Translated that and taught it years ago
> And I see: Pound was an axe,
> Chen was an axe, I am an axe
> And my son a handle, soon
> To be shaping again, model
> And tool, craft of culture,
> How we go on.

ELIOT WEINBERGER

Eliot Weinberger's books of essays include *Works on Paper* (NDP627), *Outside Stories* (NDP751), and *Karmic Traces* (NDP908). He is the author of a study of Chinese poetry translation, *19 Ways of Looking at Wang Wei*, and a collection of recent political articles, *9/12*, and the editor of the anthology *American Poetry Since 1950: Innovators & Outsiders*. His many translations of the work of Octavio Paz include the *Collected Poems 1957–1987* (NDP719), *In Light of India*, *Sunstone* (NDP735), and *A Tale of Two Gardens* (NDP841). Among his other translations are Vicente Huidobro's *Altazor*, Xavier Villaurrutia's *Nostalgia for Death*, Jorge Luis Borges' *Selected Non-Fictions* and *Seven Nights* (NDP576), and *Unlock* by Bei Dao (NDP901).